IERI Monograph Series

Issues and Methodologies in Large-Scale Assessments

VOLUME 1

IERI
IEA ETS

October 2008

A joint publication between the International Association for the Evaluation of Educational Achievement (IEA) and Educational Testing Service (ETS)

ISBN 978-0-88685-402-7

Copies of this publication can be obtained from:

IERInstitute
IEA Data Processing and Research Center
Mexikoring 37
22297 Hamburg,
Germany

IERInstitute
Educational Testing Service
Mail Stop 02-R
Princeton, NJ 08541,
United States

By email: ierinstitute@iea-dpc.de
Free downloads: www.ierinstitute.org

Copyedited by Paula Wagemaker Editorial Services, Christchurch, New Zealand
Design and production by Becky Bliss Design and Production, Wellington, New Zealand

IERI Monograph Series

Issues and Methodologies in Large-Scale Assessments

Volume 1	2008

TABLE OF CONTENTS

Introduction

Hans Wagemaker
International Association for the Evaluation of Educational Achievement, the Netherlands

Irwin Kirsch
Educational Testing Service, United States

The International Association for the Evaluation of Educational Achievement and Educational Testing Service are very pleased to establish the IERI Monograph Series, which focuses on large-scale assessment. While the history of large-scale assessment dates back at least 50 years, the last two decades have seen a significant increase in the number of these national and international assessments and their importance to policy-makers and researchers around the world. The demands of extending the application of large-scale assessment technologies to new subject matter areas as well as to an increasing diversity of countries whose linguistic, economic, and cultural circumstances are vastly different have challenged developers, methodologists, and psychometricians to create solutions that are as reliable as they are elegant.

The purpose of this publication is to contribute to the science of large-scale assessment by providing a forum through which the scientific and methodological issues related to the design and implementation of large-scale assessments can be examined. This first volume contains six insightful papers submitted by researchers from around the world. Although diverse in subject and scope, they have each been evaluated and judged to make a significant contribution to the area of large-scale assessment.

The IEA-ETS Research Institute (IERI) is a collaborative effort between the Research and Development Division at ETS and the IEA Data Processing and Research Center that focuses on improving the science of large-scale assessments. In support of this goal, IERI undertakes activities around three broad areas of work that include research studies related to the following: development and implementation of large-scale assessments; professional development and training; and dissemination of research findings and information gathered through large-scale assessments. IERI, in collaboration with interested researchers worldwide, undertakes research activities that address issues surrounding large-scale assessments, including IEA-TIMSS, IEA-PIRLS, IEA-Civics, IEA-SITES, OECD-PISA, US-NAEP, IALS, ALL, and OECD-PIAAC.

IERI is managed by an executive committee. The committee is responsible for reviewing and monitoring the progress of the collaboration; assigning work that needs to be completed to ensure a successful collaboration consistent with IERI's mission; considering work for publication in accordance with the mission; and establishing and maintaining the overall vision, goals, and business objectives of IERI. The executive committee is comprised of members from ETS and IEA. The members are, in alphabetical order, Eugenio Gonzalez (ETS), Dirk Hastedt (IEA), Juliane Hencke (IEA), Irwin Kirsch (ETS), Oliver Neuschmidt (IEA), Matthias von Davier (ETS), Hans Wagemaker (IEA), and Kentaro Yamamoto (ETS). It is co-chaired by Irwin Kirsch and Hans Wagemaker. Eugenio Gonzalez is the primary coordinator and director of the institute. As such, he has overall responsibility for managing the collaboration and activities of IERI.

Much of the research conducted through IERI may be characterized by its "virtual" nature in that research projects are hosted in diverse institutions but facilitated through web-based collaboration and the expertise of researchers from those institutes who are involved in work on large-scale assessments.

Projects undertaken through the mechanism of virtual collaboration are those that focus on one or more of the following five research priorities:

1. Use of a more systematic and scientific approach to the development, use, and interpretability of background questionnaires;
2. Development of new constructs that extend the policy issues that might be addressed by these assessments;
3. Improvement in the measurement of cognitive domains;
4. Investigation of the effects of an increased emphasis on the role and use of technology; and
5. Identification and exploration of thematic issues to guide secondary analyses of existing data.

These five areas were selected for several reasons. First, they are highly relevant to the existing surveys whose data are publicly available. Second, the findings will inform future developments and provide direction to upcoming assessments. And, third, the research will contribute to enhancing the quality and interpretability of the data. Our expectation is that helping to coordinate what is known about large-scale assessments and to promote new ideas and knowledge will ultimately enhance the visibility and utility of these assessments worldwide.

The articles published in this monograph series will feature not only work that has been funded or commissioned by IERI but also contributions from other researchers that have been submitted to the institute for publication. Work published as part of this monograph series is subject to a peer review process. Contributions are actively sought from researchers and scholars who share an interest in the advancement and use of large-scale surveys.

In publishing this first volume, we want to give special thanks to the authors and external reviewers who volunteered their time to make this publication possible.

ABOUT THE IEA

The International Association for the Evaluation of Educational Achievement (IEA) is an independent, non-profit, international cooperative of national research institutions and governmental research agencies. Through its comparative research and assessment projects, IEA aims to:

- Provide international benchmarks that may assist policy-makers identify the comparative strengths and weaknesses of their education systems;

- Provide high-quality data that will increase policy-makers' understanding of key school-based and non-school-based factors that influence teaching and learning;

- Provide high-quality data that will serve as a resource for identifying areas of concern and action, and for preparing and evaluating educational reforms;

- Develop and improve the capacity of educational systems to engage in national strategies for educational monitoring and improvement; and

- Contribute to development of the worldwide community of researchers in educational evaluation.

Additional information about IEA is available at www.iea.nl and www.iea-dpc.de.

ABOUT ETS

ETS is a non-profit institution whose mission is to advance quality and equity in education by providing fair and valid assessments, research, and related services for all people worldwide. In serving individuals, educational institutions and government agencies around the world, ETS customizes solutions to meet the need for teacher professional development products and services, classroom and end-of-course assessments, and research-based teaching and learning tools. Founded in 1947, ETS today develops, administers, and scores more than 24 million tests annually in more than 180 countries, at over 9,000 locations worldwide.

Additional information about ETS is available at www.ets.org.

Test-taking motivation on low-stakes tests: A Swedish TIMSS 2003 example

Hanna Eklöf

Department of Educational Measurement, Umeå University, Sweden

The study's objective was to investigate the test-taking motivation of students in the Swedish TIMSS 2003 context. Swedish Grade 8 students formed the study sample, and the focus was on mathematics. Test-taking motivation was measured using self-report measures (Likert-scale and open-ended questionnaire items), and reported level of test-taking motivation was regressed on test score. The quantitative part of the questionnaire study showed that the Swedish students in general reported that they were well motivated to do their best in TIMSS. According to regression analysis, test-taking motivation was positively and significantly, although rather weakly, related to mathematics achievement. Qualitative analysis of an open-ended questionnaire item mainly corroborated obtained findings but added some complexity to the results. In their answers to the open-ended item, most students reported they were well motivated to do their best in TIMSS and that they valued a good performance. Many students reported competitive, comparative, or social-responsibility reasons as motivating, while other students seemed more intrinsically motivated to do their best. Findings from quantitative as well as qualitative analyses suggest that the Swedish mathematics result in TIMSS 2003 is unlikely to be negatively affected by a lack of student motivation. However, nothing is known about student test-taking motivation in other countries participating in TIMSS, and further research exploring this issue in an international context is warranted.

INTRODUCTION

This paper presents parts of a research project being conducted on the Swedish dataset from the Trends in Mathematics and Science Study (TIMSS) 2003. The project is exploring different aspects of student achievement motivation from a measurement perspective and a validity perspective (Eklöf, 2006a, 2006b, 2007).

Student motivation is an important issue in educational settings, as achievement motivation is assumed to interact with achievement behavior in important ways (Pintrich & Schunk, 2002; Wigfield & Eccles, 2002). Achievement motivation can be conceptualized and measured on different levels of generality. The most common type of motivational measure is domain-specific and measures achievement motivation for a particular domain (e.g., mathematics, science). However, achievement motivation can also be conceptualized and measured on a situation-specific level, that is, motivation to perform well in a given situation or on a given test. Situation-specific motivation or test-taking motivation is the focus of the present paper.

A positive motivational disposition toward a test is often assumed to be a necessary though not sufficient condition for good test performance (Cronbach, 1988; Robitaille & Garden, 1996; Wainer, 1993; Zeidner, 1993). Messick (1988) noted that poor test performance could be interpreted not only in terms of test content and student ability but also in terms of lack of motivation. If different groups of students differ systematically in level of motivation, and if less motivated students are disadvantaged in that they score below their actual proficiency level, then test-taking motivation is a possible source of bias (Baumert & Demmrich, 2001; Mislevy, 1995; O'Leary, 2002; O'Neil, Sugrue, Abedi, Baker, & Golan, 1997; Robitaille & Garden, 1996; Wainer, 1993; Wise & Kong, 2005; Zeidner, 1993) and is hence a threat to the validity of score interpretation and use (Messick, 1995).

The issue of student test-taking motivation thus is an issue of validity and of the trustworthiness of test results. However, knowledge of how individuals perceive the tests they are designated to complete, and their motivation to do their best on these tests, is relatively scarce (Baumert & Demmrich, 2001; Nevo & Jäger, 1993), not least in the context of large-scale, comparative studies.

Test-Taking Motivation and Low-Stakes Tests

Tests that have no personal consequences for the test-taker, that is, low-stakes tests, have been assumed—and in some cases shown to be—associated with a decrease in motivation and performance (Wise & DeMars, 2005; Wolf & Smith, 1995; Wolf, Smith, & Birnbaum, 1995). TIMSS is, in several aspects, a low-stakes test, and the issue of test-taking motivation is therefore highly relevant in the TIMSS context. Indeed, a rather common, though rarely empirically tested, concern in the TIMSS context is that not all students are motivated to do their best on the test and that the results therefore can be an underestimation of student knowledge (Baumert & Demmrich, 2001).

The result on the TIMSS test has no impact on student grades in mathematics or science. Also, the results in TIMSS are mainly summarized at a national level and individual results are not given to the students or the schools. Thus, the students and their teachers, parents, and peers never know the result for an individual student. However, one may argue that the fact that the students represent their country in a world-wide comparative study is motivating for the students. One may also argue that the low stakes of the test make the students less anxious, and that they therefore achieve as well as they would on an ordinary test, even though they are not maximally motivated.

Previous Research on Test-Taking Motivation

A vast amount of research has investigated various aspects of general and domain-specific achievement motivation. The research on situation-specific motivation or test-taking motivation is anything but vast. Studies are scattered in time and place, as well as theoretically and methodologically. The results from earlier studies focusing on test-taking motivation have been somewhat inconclusive, and, in some cases, the link between reported level of motivation and actual achievement has been weak. Studies have found that students are quite motivated even when the test is low stakes for them (Center for Educational Testing and Evaluation, 2001), that raising the stakes does not always contribute to a corresponding rise in motivation and achievement (Baumert & Demmrich, 2001; O'Neil, Abedi, Miyoshi, & Mastergeorge, 2005), and that reported level of test-taking motivation is weakly associated with subsequent performance (O'Neil et al., 2005; Zeidner, 1993).

However, according to a number of other studies, the stakes of the test do have an impact on motivation and performance (Chan, Schmitt, DeShon, Clause, & Delbridge, 1997; Sundre & Kitsantas, 2004; Wise & DeMars, 2005; Wolf & Smith, 1995; Wolf et al., 1995). Brown and Walberg (1993) found that raising the stakes of the test by giving special instructions (emphasizing the importance of doing well and telling the students the test results were to be used for evaluation) raised the typical student's test score from the 50th to the 62nd percentile. Further, in a summary of 12 studies investigating the effects of student test-taking motivation on test performance, Wise and DeMars (2005) found that well-motivated students outperformed less-motivated students with an average effect size exceeding half a standard deviation. Wise and DeMars (2005) were also able to show a near zero correlation between self-reports of test-taking motivation and measures of ability (as measured by SAT scores), a finding that suggests there was no confounding of motivation and ability.

As far as is known, no one has tried to study student test-taking motivation in the actual context of a large-scale study like TIMSS. It is therefore unclear if the validity of the tests used in TIMSS has been compromised by a lack of motivation among the participants. We do not know if (a) the participating students lacked motivation, and/or (b) the rated level of test-taking motivation correlated with test performance. The present study explores these issues in a Swedish TIMSS 2003 context. Note that because only Swedish TIMSS participants are considered in the present study, no comparisons between countries can be made at this point.

Study Objective

The main objectives of the present study were (a) to investigate the reported level of test-taking motivation and the relationship between test-taking motivation and mathematics test performance, and (b) to explore student perceptions of test stakes and task value by analyzing data from a sample of the Swedish Grade 8 students who participated in TIMSS 2003.

METHOD

Participants

A sample (n = 343) of the Swedish Grade 8 students who participated in TIMSS 2003 took part in the present study. The sample consisted of 174 boys (50.7%) and 169 girls (49.3%). Approximately half the sample was 14 years old at the time of testing; the other half was 15 years old. Students came from 17 classes that participated in TIMSS. The classes sampled to participate were in schools monitored by national quality control observers during the administration of the TIMSS test (see Gonzalez & Diaconu, 2004). The sampling of schools was done to ensure a regional spread and a mixture of urban and rural and large and small schools. A previous study based on the same sample of students showed that the present sample was representative of the Swedish TIMSS 2003 participants (Eklöf, 2006a).

Measures of Test-Taking Motivation

Quantitative as well as qualitative measures of student test-taking motivation were obtained. The respective measures are presented below (see Eklöf, 2006b, for a detailed study design).

a) The Test-Taking Motivation Questionnaire

Because no established measures of test-taking motivation were available, and because the TIMSS test battery had no items that asked about test-taking motivation, I developed a test-taking motivation questionnaire and applied it in the Swedish TIMSS context (see Eklöf, 2006a, for a description of the development and validation of this questionnaire). I used Eccles and Wigfield's Expectancy-value Model of Achievement Motivation (Eccles & Wigfield, 2002; Pintrich & De Groot, 1990; Wigfield & Eccles, 2002) as the general theoretical basis when developing the questionnaire.

The questionnaire was administered before the students completed the TIMSS test booklet. The questionnaire consisted of 24 items, 20 of which pertained to student motivation and general attitudes toward school, mathematics, and science (19 Likert-scale items and one open-ended item; see below). Five items in the questionnaire concerned student mathematics test-taking motivation, and three of these items were associated with a common factor according to factor analysis (see below). It is important to note that because the Test-Taking Motivation Questionnaire is a newly developed instrument, it and the scale used are somewhat tentative and need ongoing development and continued validation.

One of the items in the questionnaire was an open-ended item that instructed the students to write down, in their own words, (a) how motivated they felt to do their best on the TIMSS test, and (b) the reason why they felt the way they did. The open-ended item was assumed to generate answers revealing something about the students' perceptions of task value and of the stakes of the TIMSS test. Using an item like this could thereby allow for a more in-depth understanding of student test-taking motivation in the TIMSS context.

b) Augmentation of the TIMSS Student Questionnaire

All students participating in TIMSS completed a questionnaire after they had finished the booklet containing the mathematics and science assessment items (see Martin, Mullis, & Chrostowski, 2004). Two items, which asked the students how motivated they had been to do their best on (respectively) the mathematics test and the science test, were added to the Swedish Student Questionnaire as national options. Because I considered a brief post-test measure of test-taking motivation desirable, and because it was not possible to administer the Test-Taking Motivation Questionnaire before as well as after the students completed the TIMSS booklets, I used these two augmented items in the analysis as post-test measures of test-taking motivation.

c) The TTM Scale

According to exploratory factor analysis on data from the present sample (see Eklöf, 2006a), four items formed a scale that could be used as a measure of mathematics test-taking motivation in the present study. These were:

- *Item 1:* How motivated are you to do your best on TIMSS mathematics items? (pretest measure)

- *Item 2:* How important is it for you to do your best in TIMSS? (pretest measure)

- *Item 3:* How much effort will you spend on answering the mathematics items in TIMSS? (pretest measure)

- *Item 4:* How motivated were you to do your best on TIMSS mathematics items? (post-test measure from the TIMSS Student Questionnaire).

Items 1 to 3 were taken from the Test-Taking Motivation Questionnaire; Item 4 was taken from the TIMSS Student Questionnaire. This four-item scale was named Test-Taking Motivation (TTM). All items in the scale were measured on a four-point scale, with ratings ranging from a highly unfavorable attitude to a highly favorable attitude (1 = *not at all motivated*, 4 = *very motivated*) (see Eklöf, 2007, for a more detailed presentation of the items in the scale).

TIMSS 2003 Mathematics Test

In the TIMSS surveys, each student completes a booklet containing only a sample of the total number of mathematics/science items used in the study. It is therefore impossible, when using raw data, to calculate a total score that can be compared over populations and sub-populations. To allow analysts to obtain comparable achievement scores, each student receives a scaled score that represents an estimation of the student's score if he or she had answered all items (see Martin et al., 2004).

Two different kinds of scores are estimated for each student. One is the national Rasch score (see Eklöf, 2007, for analyses of the relationship between test-taking motivation and test performance using the Rasch score as the dependent variable). The other score consists of five "plausible values" for each student. These values are imputed values obtained through complex item-response modeling. The five values an individual obtains are random excerpts from the distribution of possible values for that individual. The mean plausible value is set to 500, with a standard deviation of 100. All achievement results reported in TIMSS internationally are based on these plausible values, and I also used the plausible values in mathematics as the dependent variable in this present study.

Quantitative Data Analysis

My first step was to compute descriptive statistics and correlations between variables using SPSS 15.0. I then regressed student ratings of test-taking motivation on the mathematics score. This regression included two motivational scales used internationally in TIMSS—mathematics self-concept (MSC) and student valuing of mathematics (VoM). These two scales are domain-specific measures of achievement motivation, in contrast to the TTM scale, which measures task-specific motivation. I held the MSC and the VoM scales constant in the regression analysis in order to determine if the test-taking motivation scale explained any variance in the mathematics score not explained by these two motivational variables. The *IEA IDB Analyzer*, a plug-in program for SPSS supplied by the IEA Data Processing and Research Center in Germany, was used to run the regressions. This program for analyzing IEA data uses all five plausible values as dependent variables and makes sure that correct sample weights are used and that standard errors are correctly calculated through the use of the jackknifing method (see Martin et al., 2004). All tests of significance were two-tailed and the alpha level was set to 0.05.

Qualitative Data Analysis

My analysis of the open-ended item in the Test-Taking Motivation Questionnaire followed a two-stage procedure. First, I categorized the student responses to the open-ended item as "positive", "negative," or "indifferent," depending on how the students expressed themselves in terms of their motivational disposition toward the TIMSS test. Second, I analyzed the reasons students gave for their motivation or lack of motivation, identified common themes in the students' responses, and joined similar responses from students in one category.

For reliability purposes, I engaged a second rater to analyze the responses to the open-ended item. This external rater was blind to my categorization but did receive a scheme containing the main categories and instructions for coding. There was a high degree of convergence between us. We disagreed on only 24 (7%) of the 329 valid responses to the open-ended item.

FINDINGS

The findings are presented as follows:

1. A description of the students' ratings on the TTM scale as well as their ratings of the individual items.

2. An account of the multiple linear regressions exploring the relationship between the TTM scale and the mathematics score, with students' ratings of mathematics self-concept and their valuing of the mathematics subject held constant.

3. A summary of the results from the open-ended item in the Test-Taking Motivation Questionnaire.

Reported Level of Test-Taking Motivation

The TTM scale had a score reliability coefficient of $\alpha = 0.79$, which is acceptable given that the scale consisted of only four items. The maximum value of the TTM scale was 4.0, and the mean value for the present sample was 3.09 ($SD = 0.55$), which indicates that the students in the sample reported on average a fairly high level of test-taking motivation.

In regard to the individual items in the TTM scale, a majority of the students in the sample ($n = 343$) reported that they were either very motivated or somewhat motivated to do their best on TIMSS mathematics items before (89%) as well as after (76%) taking the test. A majority of the students said that it was either very important or somewhat important for them to do their best in TIMSS (74%), and that they would spend a lot of effort or a fair amount of effort (90%) when answering the TIMSS mathematics tasks (see Eklöf, 2007, for more detailed results).

Relationships between Ratings of Test-Taking Motivation and Mathematics Score

For the total sample, the TTM scale positively but rather weakly correlated with the mathematics score ($r = 0.25$, $p < 0.01$). As noted above, investigation of whether the TTM scale accounted for any variation in the TIMSS mathematics score when other relevant variables were held constant required building a regression model in which the TTM scale and the two motivational scales used internationally in TIMSS—that is, mathematics self-concept (MSC) and student valuing of mathematics (VoM)—were independent variables.

According to this model, the three independent variables together explained about 42% (R^2) of the variation in the mathematics score for the present sample. Most of this variation was explained by the MSC variable ($\beta = 71.34$, $SE = 5.91$, $t = 12.06$, $p < 0.01$). The TTM variable had a positive and statistically significant, though rather weak, relationship to the mathematics score when the other independent variables were partialed out ($\beta = 11.76$, $SE = 4.78$, $t = 2.46$, $p < 0.05$). The VoM variable was not related to the mathematics score when the effect of the other independent variables was partialed out ($\beta = -7.60$, $SE = 6.41$, $t = -0.44$, $p = $ n.s.).

The Open-Ended Item

There were 329 valid responses to the open-ended item (96% of the total number). During the first phase of analysis, I coded student answers as "positive," "negative," or "indifferent" in terms of motivational disposition toward the TIMSS test. According to this analysis, 238 (72%) of the 329 students expressed themselves in positive terms concerning their participation in TIMSS and their motivation to do their best. Forty-eight students (15%) expressed a rather indifferent attitude, and 43 students (13%) reported a negative motivational disposition toward the TIMSS test.

The second phase involved analyzing the students' explanations as to why they felt motivated or not. I grouped the students reporting a positive motivational disposition toward the TIMSS test in their answers to the open-ended item into four major categories:

- *Category 1:* The students in this category expressed a *social responsibility/ comparative perspective* as the main reason for wanting to do their best. These students wanted to do their best because they had been chosen for this study; they wanted to do their best to help with the research; and they wanted to do their best because so many countries were to be compared.

- *Category 2:* Here, the students mainly gave *competitive reasons* for their motivation to do well. They wanted to show that Sweden is a prominent country, and they wanted to "win this competition."

- *Category 3:* The students in this category mainly gave *personal, intrinsic* reasons for their motivation to do well. They said they always did their best in order to feel good about themselves, and they wanted to do their best to test themselves—to see how much they knew.

- *Category 4:* In this category, students reported that they felt motivated simply because it was "*fun*" or "*interesting*" to participate in the study.

The first two, slightly overlapping, categories thus consisted of students reporting mainly extrinsic factors as motivating. The latter two categories consisted of students referring to mainly intrinsic factors as motivating.

Among the students who claimed that they were not well motivated to do their best, two further categories could be identified. The first included students who reported the *low stakes* of the test as the reason why they did not feel maximally motivated (the result did not count for their grades; they would never know the results). The second group of students reported that they were not motivated because they *did not like school, the school subjects tested*, or *tests in general*. Also, a fair number of students could not be placed in any of the above categories, either because they gave reasons that did not easily fit into these categories or because they did not give any particular reason for their motivation or lack of motivation. Table 1 shows the number of students placed within each category.

It is important to note here that 30 students from the sample used in the present study also agreed to be interviewed about their perceptions of the TIMSS test. The interview results corroborated, to a high degree, the results from the analysis of the open-ended item, which adds credibility to the findings from the questionnaire study (for detailed findings from these interviews, see Eklöf, 2006b).

Table 1: Student explanations for why they felt motivated/not motivated to do their best on the TIMSS test according to their answers to the open-ended questionnaire item (*n* = 329)

Primary reason given	*n*	%	Examples of student answers
Personal/Intrinsic	58	18	*I want to do my best to see how much I have learned over the years.*
Fun/Interesting	39	12	*I feel very motivated to do this test. I feel no pressure, but it feels fun to do it.*
Comparative/Social Responsibility	84	26	*I am motivated to do my best. I think it is an important test to see how children in different parts of the world work and how they solve problems.*
Competitive	38	12	*I am fairly motivated to do my best, as it is a competition. And you'd rather win.*
Low stakes of the test	31	9	*Not particularly motivated, as it doesn't affect my grades.*
Dislike school subjects/Tests in general	12	3	*Not very motivated, as I don't like math and science.*
Various other reasons/No reason given	67	21	*I don't have to go to English class.*

SUMMARY AND CONCLUDING REMARKS

The main purpose of the work presented in this paper was to study student test-taking motivation in the TIMSS 2003 context. Few studies, if any, have investigated student test-taking motivation in the actual context of a large-scale, international comparative study like TIMSS. The issue of test-taking motivation on low-stakes tests is an issue about validity and about the trustworthiness of test results. As such, it is an issue worthy of attention in the context of large-scale, comparative studies.

Two main conclusions can be drawn from the obtained results. First, the quantitative as well as the qualitative analyses indicate that the Swedish students participating in TIMSS 2003 were generally well motivated to do their best on the TIMSS test and that they valued a good performance on the test. Second, the Swedish mathematics result in TIMSS 2003 does not seem to have been affected by a lack of motivation among the participating students for two reasons. First, most of the students reported that they were well motivated to do their best, and second, ratings of test-taking motivation related weakly to test performance. In essence, the obtained results indicate that TIMSS mathematics scores for Swedish students were minimally biased by test-taking motivation and so can be interpreted as representing mathematics knowledge.

The results obtained in the present study do not support findings from a number of previous studies that report test stakes influence motivation and performance, and that low-stakes tests are associated with a low level of test-taking motivation as well as a lower than expected performance. Students in the present sample did not report a low level of test-taking motivation, probably because most students did not perceive the TIMSS test as a low-stakes test in the sense that it was unimportant and not worth spending effort on. Some students reported they were intrinsically motivated to do their best while other students reported they were extrinsically motivated, for example by the fact that they were representing Sweden in a study where countries would be compared with one another. The students who did report the low stakes of the test as detrimental to their motivation constituted a minority of the total sample.

It is noteworthy that children in Grade 8 in the current Swedish education system have little experience of extensive testing in school. They are therefore not used to lengthy, standardized tests like those used in TIMSS. Further, these students do not receive grades for their schoolwork until they are in Grade 8. Therefore, Swedish eighth-graders are not "fed up" with testing and assessment, and this might explain their positive attitude toward doing the "non-consequential" TIMSS test. Also, the importance of doing well on a test like TIMSS has to be accentuated by someone, and it seems that the Swedish teachers and school leaders had succeeded in informing the students about TIMSS and in motivating the students to do their best.

Even if the test-taking motivation scale used in the present study seems psychometrically sound (see Eklöf, 2006a), it is important to acknowledge that the scale is a newly developed self-report scale, that the properties of the scale have not been extensively validated, and that the results depend on the honesty of the respondents. The low correlation between test-taking motivation scores and mathematics achievement may possibly be due to an inability of the scale to capture relevant aspects of student test-taking motivation. The restriction of range in the TTM variable, and the resulting ceiling effect, may also have contributed to the weak association between test-taking motivation and achievement. Future studies are needed to further the development of the TTM scale.

An obvious limitation of the present paper is that the study includes only Swedish TIMSS participants and that it therefore is not possible to study potential bias in the international comparisons due to varying levels of test-taking motivation. Nothing is known about student test-taking motivation in other countries participating in TIMSS and in other large-scale, international studies. Level of test-taking motivation may well differ between countries and cultures. Cross-country comparisons of test-taking motivation and of the effect of test-taking motivation on test achievement therefore constitute an important area of future research. Other systematic group differences in test-taking motivation such as age differences, gender differences, and differences between ethnic and social groups in national and international contexts are also worthy of systematic investigation.

The present paper also illustrates the possibility for each participating country to add (or adapt) national options to the TIMSS test battery. The findings of this present study and the lack of research overall relative to the issues discussed in this paper strongly suggest that more nations, or possibly collaborating clusters of nations, should take advantage of this possibility. Moreover, because nations participating in TIMSS have unique characteristics, adding national options to the anchor instruments administered by TIMSS could allow mirroring of these unique characteristics and enable large-scale investigation of questions of particular interest. It would also be possible to include a measure that combines student effort, perceived importance of a good performance, and/or level of motivation in the TIMSS test battery. Including such a measure could contribute not only to our understanding of score meaning but also to the validity of score-based inferences.

References

Baumert, J., & Demmrich, A. (2001). Test motivation in the assessment of student skills: The effects of incentives on motivation and performance. *European Journal of Psychology of Education, 16*, 441–462.

Brown, S. M., & Wahlberg, H. J. (1993). Motivational effects on test scores of elementary students. *Journal of Educational Research, 86*, 133–136.

Center for Educational Testing and Evaluation. (2001). *Student test taking motivation and performance: Grade 10 mathematics and science and Grade 11 social studies* (research report). Lawrence, KS: School of Education, University of Kansas.

Chan, D., Schmitt, N., DeShon, R. P., Clause, C. S., & Delbridge, K. (1997). Reactions to cognitive ability tests: The relationships between race, test performance, face validity perceptions, and test-taking motivation. *Journal of Applied Psychology, 82*, 300–310.

Cronbach, L. J. (1988). Five perspectives on validity argument. In H. Wainer & H. I. Braun (Eds.), *Test validity* (pp. 3–17). Hillsdale, NJ: Erlbaum.

Eccles, J. S., & Wigfield, A. (2002). Motivational beliefs, values, and goals. *Annual Review of Psychology, 53*, 109–132.

Eklöf, H. (2006a). Development and validation of scores from an instrument measuring student test-taking motivation. *Educational and Psychological Measurement, 66*, 643–656.

Eklöf, H. (2006b). *Motivational beliefs in the TIMSS 2003 context: Theory, measurement and relation to test performance*. Unpublished doctoral dissertation, Department of Educational Measurement, Umeå University, Umeå.

Eklöf, H. (2007). Test-taking motivation and mathematics performance in TIMSS 2003. *International Journal of Testing, 7*, 311–326.

Gonzalez, E., & Diaconu, D. (2004). Quality assurance in the TIMSS 2003 data collection. In M. Martin, I. V. S. Mullis, & S. J. Chrostowski (Eds.), *TIMSS 2003 technical report* (pp. 142–171). Chestnut Hill, MA: Boston College.

Martin, M. O., Mullis, I. V. S., & Chrostowski, S. J. (2004). *TIMSS 2003 technical report*. Chestnut Hill, MA: Boston College.

Messick, S. (1988). The once and future issues of validity: Assessing the meaning and consequences of measurement. In H. Wainer & H. I. Braun (Eds.), *Test validity* (pp. 33–46). Hillsdale, NJ: Lawrence Erlbaum.

Messick, S. (1995). Validity of psychological assessment: Validation of inferences from persons' responses and performance as scientific inquiry into score meaning. *American Psychologist, 50*, 741–749.

Mislevy, R. J. (1995). What can we learn from international assessments? *Educational Evaluation and Policy Analysis, 4*, 419–437.

Nevo, B., & Jäger, R. S. (1993). *Educational and psychological testing: The test taker's outlook*. Stuttgart: Hogrefe & Huber Publishers.

O'Leary, M. (2002). Stability of country rankings across item formats in the Third International Mathematics and Science Study. *Educational Measurement: Issues and Practice, 21*, 27–38.

O'Neil, H. F., Abedi, J., Miyoshi, J., & Mastergeorge, A. (2005). Monetary incentives for low-stakes tests. *Educational Assessment, 10*, 185–208.

O'Neil, H. F., Sugrue, B., Abedi, J., Baker, E. L., & Golan, S. (1997). *Final report of experimental studies on motivation and NAEP test performance* (CSE Technical Report 427). Los Angeles, CA: CRESST, University of California.

Pintrich, P. R., & De Groot, E. V. (1990). Motivational and self-regulated learning components of classroom academic performance. *Journal of Educational Psychology, 82*, 33–40.

Pintrich, P. R., & Schunk, D. H. (2002). *Motivation in education: Theory, research, and applications* (2nd ed.). New Jersey, NJ: Merrill Prentice Hall.

Robitaille, D. F., & Garden, R. A. (1996). *Research questions and study design* (TIMSS Monograph No. 2). Vancouver: Pacific Educational Press.

Sundre, D. L., & Kitsantas, A. (2004). An exploration of the psychology of the examinee: Can examinee self-regulation and test-taking motivation predict consequential and non-consequential test performance? *Contemporary Educational Psychology, 29*, 6–26.

Wainer, H. (1993). Measurement problems. *Journal of Educational Measurement, 30*, 1–21.

Wigfield, A., & Eccles, J. (2002). The development of competence beliefs, expectancies for success, and achievement values from childhood through adolescence. In A. Wigfield & J. Eccles (Eds.), *Development of achievement motivation* (pp. 92–120). New York: Academic Press.

Wise, S. L., & DeMars, C. (2005). Low examinee effort in low-stakes assessment: Problems and possible solutions. *Educational Assessment, 10*, 1–17.

Wise, S. L., & Kong, X. (2005). Response time effort: A new measure of examinee motivation in computer-based tests. *Applied Measurement in Education, 18*, 163–183.

Wolf, L. F., & Smith, J. K. (1995). The consequence of consequence: Motivation, anxiety, and test performance. *Applied Measurement in Education, 8*, 227–242.

Wolf, L. F., Smith, J. K., & Birnbaum, M. E. (1995). Consequence of performance, test motivation, and mentally taxing items. *Applied Measurement in Education, 8*, 341–351.

Zeidner, M. (1993). Essay versus multiple-choice-type classroom exams: The student's perspective. In B. Nevo & R. S. Jäger (Eds.), *Educational and psychological testing: The test taker's outlook* (pp. 85–111). Stuttgart: Hogrefe & Huber Publishers.

An alternative examination of Chinese Taipei mathematics achievement: Application of the rule-space method to TIMSS 1999 data

Yi-Hsin Chen
University of South Florida, Tampa, Florida, United States of America

Joanna S. Gorin and Marilyn S. Thompson
Arizona State University, Tempe, Arizona, United States of America

Kikumi K. Tatsuoka
Columbia University, New York, United States of America

Rule-space methodology employing a well-designed cognitive model validated for the Chinese Taipei TIMSS 1999 sample of Grade 8 students was used to produce a diagnostic description of these students' cognitive abilities and skills relative to the TIMSS assessment items. The study also looked at the students' distribution across identified knowledge states. Using a mastery probability cut-off criterion of 0.85 for the 23 previously established attributes, the researchers determined that the Chinese Taipei students, as a group, had not mastered five attributes, including number sense, approximation and estimation, recognizing patterns, logical reasoning, and quantitative and logical reading. The descriptions of cognitive attributes suggest that Chinese Taipei students have somewhat weak high-level mathematical thinking skills compared to their other mastery attributes. Twelve clustered knowledge states were identified from all individual knowledge states and were categorized into four performance levels. Some suggestions based on the cognitive diagnostic information provided by this study are linked to the Chinese Taipei educational context and instructional practices.

INTRODUCTION

It is reasonable to assume that the primary goal of standardized educational assessment is to obtain information on student learning so as to improve it (Linn, 1989). Clear definitions of what constitutes student learning are therefore critical. One means by which educators define learning is through the use of behavioral objectives that specify the types of behavior an individual is expected to perform. Because the majority of behaviors in classrooms center on problem-solving or other mental functions, objectives are often phrased in terms of cognitive processes. Research that analyzes test results explicitly in terms of cognitive processes therefore is timely.

Although test scores are generally presented as "the number correct" or as a scale score, they are nonetheless useful measures of learning to the extent that they measure the cognitive processes represented by the tasks on the test. Unfortunately, the traditional psychometric models that underlie most educational tests (notably those based on classical test theory or item response theory) do not reflect the *cognitive* information embedded in test scores (Snow & Lohman, 1989). As Embretson (1993) has observed, "although the item response theory models that are typically applied have many advantages over earlier testing methods, they have little connection with the concerns of cognitive theory about the processes, strategies, and knowledge structures that underlie item solving" (p. 125). Thus, one of the greatest limitations of traditional psychometric models is that they provide only external estimates of student performance on tests, such as total scores or theta estimates, rather than internal information regarding what knowledge or skills students actually possess as evidenced by correct answers. The restriction exists primarily because traditional psychometric models are limited on cognitive grounds (Herman, 1991; Snow & Lohman, 1989). The deficiency of cognitive information available from traditional ability estimates in turn limits the utility of the tests as a means of diagnostic feedback to instructors in classrooms. As a result, achievement tests tend to be used for selection, placement, and certification purposes, rather than for diagnosing student strengths and weaknesses.

Having recognized the potential benefits of cognitive analysis, a number of researchers have combined cognitive information with modern psychometric models in order to fulfill various educational assessment purposes. Examinees' responses are still important within each of these approaches, but they are not dominant. The models, which collectively, as Stout (2002) maintains, can be conceptualized as skills-based (i.e., cognitive-based), include the following: Fischer's (1973) logistic latent-trait model (LLTM); Embretson's (1984, 1985) series of multidimensional, continuous-trait, non-compensatory logistic IRT models; Tatsuoka's (1983, 1990, 1995) rule-space method; and Mislevy's (1994) Bayes Net Approach. Although these methods differ in their major goals and estimation approaches, they all have one feature in common—the addition of cognitive information (Embretson & Gorin, 2001; Embretson & Reise, 2000; Gorin, 2002). In this paper, we take a closer look at one of these approaches— the rule-space method (RSM)—in relation to data from TIMSS 1999 (also known as TIMSS-Repeat or TIMSS-R).

The Rule-Space Method

Developed by K. K. Tatsuoka (1983, 1990, 1995), the rule-space method (RSM) is a mathematically probabilistic approach to analyzing test data that involves incorporating cognitive skills-based information into psychometric models. In addition to taking account of the traditional ability estimate provided for each examinee, the RSM diagnoses the cognitive attributes of individuals and groups of students according to their patterns of responses on a test. Attributes include knowledge, skills, and the processing abilities required to successfully solve a test problem (Birenbaum, Kelly, & Tatsuoka, 1993). The approach taken when describing them is very similar to that for behavioral objectives. RSM thus provides a diagnostic profile for an individual or a group that is based on their mastery or non-mastery of the cognitive attributes underlying the items of a test. Each particular pattern of mastery or non-mastery of attributes relative to a test is known within RSM terminology as the individual's or group's "knowledge state" (Tatsuoka & Tatsuoka, 1987), and each examinee is assigned, based on his or her responses to the test items, to one of several predetermined knowledge states. The RSM model, therefore, is predicated on the assumption that examinees' performance on a task or a test can be directly tied to the knowledge, skills, and processing abilities required for successful task completion that each examinee personally has at hand (Everson, Guerrero, & Yamada, 2003).

RSM comprises two main phases that together include four steps (Tatsuoka, 1995; Tatsuoka & Boodoo, 2000):

- *Phase 1, determination of latent knowledge states:* The two steps in this phase involve (i) identifying unobservable cognitive attributes in a domain of interest and creating the incidence matrix (also known as the Q-matrix), and (ii) determining ideal latent knowledge states (the ideal item-response patterns or classification groups).

- *Phase 2, classification of examinees' knowledge states:* The steps here require (iii) mapping the observed response patterns into the ideal item-response patterns, and (iv) classifying each examinee's responses into the most appropriate knowledge state.

The Q-matrix of the first step depicts the relationships between required cognitive attributes and test items. The list of cognitive attributes and the Q-matrix are thus seen as a representation of the cognitive model used in the rule-space analyses, and it is this incidence matrix that provides the reference point during application of Boolean Descriptive Functions (BDF) in order to determine all possible latent knowledge states (Tatsuoka, 1991). The *predetermined* latent knowledge state, also called an attribute mastery pattern, is expressed as an attribute pattern consisting of a list of the mastered/non-mastered attributes that an examinee uses (Tatsuoka & Boodoo, 2000). Because the latent knowledge states are represented by binary patterns of cognitive attributes that cannot be observed directly, the BDF plays a linking role by setting out these unobservable knowledge states as observable ideal item-response patterns. These patterns, within the context of RSM, are regarded as classification groups.

After identifying the ideal item-response patterns, analysts then compare the examinees' item-response patterns against the *ideal* item-response patterns in order to classify the examinees into one of the predetermined knowledge states. From here, Mahalanobis distances between examinees' response patterns and the ideal response patterns are calculated, and a Bayesian decision rule is used to determine which of several ideal response patterns best matches each examinee's response patterns. Once an individual examinee has been classified into a knowledge state, information regarding his or her mastered/non-mastered attributes is available as useful learning feedback for both examinee and instructor.

The Cognitive Attribute Model Prepared for the TIMSS 1999 Mathematics Test

Corter and Tatsuoka (2002) generated a set of the cognitive knowledge and processing skills underlying performance on the TIMSS 1999 mathematics test. They used three sources of data to create this set: the content and performance frameworks used for the TIMSS 1995 and the TIMSS 1999 mathematics tests (Gonzalez & Miles, 2001); a proposed set of attributes assumed to explain performance on SAT and GRE mathematics items (Tatsuoka, 1995; Tatsuoka & Boodoo, 2000); and written protocols from domain experts. The researchers also validated these attributes by interviewing several students and high school mathematics teachers and by conducting statistical analyses of the TIMSS 1999 sample for the United States (Corter & Tatsuoka, 2002).

To develop the Q-matrix (i.e., to establish the relationships between attributes and test items), the two researchers and one doctoral student independently coded each of the 162 test items according to its identified attributes. They then discussed any differences in coding with one another and reviewed the student protocols in order to reach consensus on the coding for each item. After obtaining an acceptable Q-matrix, the researchers made a series of improvements to it by using statistical approaches such as multiple regression and correlations among attributes until they created what they deemed to be a valid and reliable incidence matrix. In addition, they prepared a manual featuring the coding for the TIMSS 1999 test-item attributes (Tatsuoka, Corter, & Guerrero, 2004). The cognitive attributes and the Q-matrix that eventually emerged from this work comprise the cognitive attribute model for the TIMSS 1999 mathematics test, and this model was the one we applied in the current study.

It is important to note that Tatsuoka and her colleagues (Tatsuoka, Guerrero, Corter, Yamada, & Tatsuoka, 2003) validated the set of cognitive attributes and the Q-matrix through reference to data from 20 of the countries that participated in TIMSS 1999. (These countries included the United States but not Chinese Taipei.) The researchers concluded that the cognitive model adequately represented eighth-graders' mathematics performance on the TIMSS 1999 tests across the 20 countries (Tatsuoka et al., 2003). They also found that the top-scoring countries in the TIMSS 1999 mathematics test (see also Mullis et al., 2000) differed in terms of how they "produced" good performance. For instance, Japanese students tended to learn mathematical thinking skills earlier than they learned content knowledge, while students from Hong Kong acquired solid content knowledge first and mathematical thinking skills later (Tatsuoka et al., 2003). We used the list of cognitive attributes and the Q-matrix validated for the Chinese Taipei sample (Chen, Gorin, Thompson, & Tatsuoka, 2008) to conduct research that might provide us with a better understanding of what a high-performing TIMSS country, such as Chinese Taipei, the third-ranking country in the study, does to educate its students to this degree of success.

Research Purpose

Our overall purpose in this present study was to apply RSM to the TIMSS 1999 mathematics achievement data for Chinese Taipei eighth-graders. We examined the knowledge states most evident among these students in order to provide better descriptive accounts of how well they performed on the TIMSS 1999 items in terms of cognitive attributes and knowledge states. To state our goal in different terms, we wanted to identify which cognitive attributes these students had mastered or not mastered. Another aim was to explore how the students "distributed" across these knowledge states. Finally, we wanted to determine if and how this cognitively diagnostic information linked to Chinese Taipei's educational context and instructional practices.

METHOD

Participants

A total of 5,772 Chinese Taipei students nested within 150 schools participated in TIMSS 1999. The sample for the current study was based on students who completed TIMSS Booklets 1, 3, 5, and 7. Our eventual sample comprised 2,874 students out of the 5,772 students tested.

Instrument

Although the TIMSS mathematics test involved eight question-and-answer booklets, the data that we used for the current study came only from those Chinese Taipei eighth-graders who completed Booklets 1, 3, 5, and 7. We selected these booklets according to the criterion that each attribute to be analyzed in the study had to be included in *at least* three items (see Corter & Tatsuoka, 2002). Note that the mathematics tests used in TIMSS 1999 involved five content categories: (i) fractions and number sense (38% of the total number of items); (ii) measurement (15%); (iii) data representation, analysis, and probability (13%); (iv) geometry (13%); and (v) algebra (22%). Item types involved multiple-choice (77%), short-answer (13%), and extended-response formats (10%) (Gonzalez & Miles, 2001).

Cognitive Attributes and Incidence Matrix

Originally, Corter and Tatsuoka (2002) classified the 27 cognitive attributes that represent the underlying performance of the TIMSS 1999 mathematics test into the three categories shown in Table 1: content knowledge (C1 to C6), cognitive processes (P1 to P10), and skill/item-type (S1 to S11). Also on the basis of previous research (Tatsuoka, Corter, & Tatsuoka, 2004), we decided to delete Attributes C6, S1, S9,

Table 1: Knowledge, skill, and process attributes underlying performance on the TIMSS 1999 mathematics test

CONTENT ATTRIBUTES	
C1	Basic concepts, properties, and operations in whole numbers and integers
C2	Basic concepts, properties, and operations in fractions and decimals
C3	Basic concepts, properties, and operations in elementary algebra
C4	Basic concepts and properties of two-dimensional geometry
C5	Data, probability, and basic statistics
C6	Using tools to measure (or estimate) length, time, angle, and temperature
PROCESS ATTRIBUTES	
P1	Translate/formulate equations and expressions to solve a problem
P2	Computational applications of knowledge in arithmetic and geometry
P3	Judgmental applications of knowledge in arithmetic and geometry
P4	Applying rules in algebra
P5	Logical reasoning such as case reasoning, deductive thinking skills, if–then, necessary and sufficient, generalization skills
P6	Problem search, analytical thinking, problem restructuring, and inductive thinking
P7	Generating, visualizing, and reading figures and graphs
P8	Applying and evaluating mathematical correctness
P9	Management of data and procedures
P10	Quantitative and logical reading
SKILL (ITEM-TYPE) ATTRIBUTES	
S1	Unit conversion
S2	Applying number properties and relationships; number sense/number line
S3	Using figures, tables, charts, and graphs
S4	Approximation/estimation
S5	Evaluate/verify/check options
S6	Patterns and relationships (able to apply inductive thinking skills)
S7	Using proportional reasoning
S8	Solving novel or unfamiliar problems
S9	Comparing two or more entities
S10	Open-ended item, in which an answer is not given
S11	Using words to communicate questions

Note: Adapted from Corter and Tatsuoka (2002, p. 18).

and P8 from the current study because these did not appear in a sufficient number of items in Booklets 1, 3, 5, and 7. We accordingly used in the current study a total of 23 initial cognitive attributes of knowledge and skills (5 content attributes, 9 process attributes, and 9 skill/item-type attributes) as an initial list of attributes for the Chinese Taipei data. Table 2 gives the frequencies of attributes required for the items in the four booklets.

Table 2: Frequencies of attributes required in items for each booklet of the TIMSS 1999 mathematics test

Attribute		Booklet 1	Booklet 3	Booklet 5	Booklet 7	Total items
C1	Whole numbers and integers	14	6	10	10	40
C2	Fractions and decimals	15	19	19	17	70
C3	Elementary algebra	10	9	4	4	27
C4	Two-dimensional geometry	13	14	10	6	43
C5	Data and basic statistics	10	6	10	7	33
S2	Number sense	8	6	5	4	23
S3	Figures, tables, and graphs	19	17	22	15	73
S4	Approximation and estimation	4	6	5	5	20
S5	Evaluate and verify options	17	11	15	17	60
S6	Recognize patterns	6	1	3	4	14
S7	Proportional reasoning	11	12	14	12	49
S8	Novel/unfamiliar problems	10	12	10	8	40
S10	Open-ended items	13	10	12	9	44
S11	Word problems	25	18	18	18	79
P1	Translate	15	16	13	13	57
P2	Computation application	17	17	19	19	72
P3	Judgmental application	9	10	7	8	34
P4	Rule application in algebra	7	9	4	4	24
P5	Logical reasoning	17	13	11	7	48
P6	Solution search	9	10	5	8	32
P7	Visual figures and graphs	13	10	13	8	44
P9	Data management	20	14	13	8	55
P10	Quantitative reading	11	6	9	10	36

After completing their first step of the work, Tatsuoka and her colleagues (Tatsuoka, Corter, & Guerrero, 2004) used the identified attribute list to construct an incidence matrix (a Q-matrix). This specified the exact relationship between the items and the cognitive processing attributes. Unlike the design framework of the TIMSS mathematics test, where each item is categorized into only one content category or one performance category, the Q-matrix that Tatsuoka and her colleagues used did not restrict selection to a specific number of attributes associated with each item (Tatsuoka, Corter, & Tatsuoka, 2004). Thus, an item could involve any number of possible attributes. For instance, one item could involve two content attributes, three process attributes, and one item-type attribute. Figure 1 provides an example of an item and its associated attributes (see also Tatsuoka, Corter, & Guerrero, 2004).

Figure 1: Example of item attribute coding on a TIMSS mathematics item

Problem: A teacher and a doctor each have 45 books. If 4/5 of the teacher's books and 2/3 of the doctor's books are novels, how many more novels does the teacher have than the doctor?

A. 2   B. 3   C. 6   D. 30   E. 36

Attributes involved in: C2, P1, P5, P9, S11

The content is fractions	$\longrightarrow$ C2
Translate the expression into arithmetic	$\longrightarrow$ P1
To understand the comparison expressed by "how many more"	$\longrightarrow$ P5
Two goals problem	$\longrightarrow$ P9
This is a verbally expressed problem	$\longrightarrow$ S11

ANALYSIS

This process involved *rule-space analyses and knowledge state analyses*. We used a special computer software program called BUGSHELL, programmed by Tatsuoka, Varadi, and Tatsuoka (1992), for the rule-space analysis, and the three-dimensional Cartesian coordinate space to formulate the classification space, which consisted of the IRT ability (θ), ζ, and generalized ζ. The variable ζ measured the extent of the unusualness of item-response patterns in the whole test (Tatsuoka, 1984), while the generalized ζ focused the extent of the unusualness on the particular subset of interest (Tatsuoka, 1996).

For the purpose of classification, we also set in advance several relevant parameters for rule-space analyses. We began by setting the acceptable Mahalanobis distance and the difference of θ values between an examinee's item-response pattern and the ideal item-response pattern to 4.5 and 1.5, respectively. Next, we set the number of slips (i.e., the number of differing responses between the observed and the ideal item patterns in the test) to comprise no more than one third of the total items (Corter & Tatsuoka, 2002). Finally, we performed a separate rule-space analysis for each booklet.

Our second main analysis, the knowledge states analysis, initially involved a large number of knowledge states because of the large samples used in the current study. In order to establish more meaningful and interpretable knowledge states for diagnostic information, similar knowledge states were grouped together into a smaller number of such states. We first merged the attribute mastery probability vectors from the four rule-space analyses into a single dataset. According to Tatsuoka, Xin, Corter, and Tatsuoka (2004), combining examinee attribute mastery probabilities derived from different booklets into a single dataset is justified by the common set of cognitive attributes underlying each booklet.

Our next step was to conduct a K-means cluster analysis that included applying several criteria in order to obtain an appropriate number of clusters. These criteria were as follows:

1. The number of classified students for each cluster should be greater than 1% of the sample size;

2. The average distance between each classified student's knowledge state and the hypothesized cluster centroid of a knowledge state should be smaller than 2.0, which means that each student's knowledge state in his or her own cluster is closely located; and

3. Observed F statistics from univariate ANOVAs conducted for each separate attribute should be high (Tatsuoka et al., 2003).

Because we selected the clusters to maximize the differences among cases in the K-mean cluster analysis, we applied only the F values for our descriptive purposes.

After obtaining the hypothesized clusters, we computed the probability estimate for each attribute in a particular cluster by averaging all mastery probabilities on one attribute across the examinees classified into that cluster. Each probability vector represented the centroid of a hypothesized cluster. Using the numeric cut-off of 0.85, we then transformed the probability vector for each cluster into the binary indicator vector, in which 0s represented non-mastery and 1s indicated mastery. (This binary vector is equivalent to the attribute mastery pattern for the clustered knowledge state.) We also calculated a single estimate of mastery probability for each cluster by averaging all of the attribute mastery probabilities in a particular clustered knowledge state.

RESULTS

We begin this section of the paper by providing examples of the attribute mastery probabilities that we obtained for several students. We then present descriptive statistics of the attribute mastery probabilities for the entire sample of Chinese Taipei eighth-graders whose data were used in the current study. The second part of this results section presents findings relating to the clustered knowledge states.

Attribute Mastery Probabilities

Individual Diagnostic Information

The most fundamental and important output from rule-space analyses is the individual diagnostic information relating to students' (both individual and whole sample or population) mastery probabilities of content and process attributes. Figure 2 provides three examples of students' item-response patterns and the corresponding attribute mastery probabilities derived from the rule-space analyses.

Figure 2: Example of students' item-response patterns and the corresponding attribute mastery probabilities

Student A
Booklet taken = 3; Total scores = 38; Percentage correct responses = 90.48;
Item-response pattern (42 items)
111111111111111111111111111011111110110011
Attribute Mastery Probability (23 attributes)

1.00	1.00	1.00	1.00	0.78
1.00	1.00	0.65	1.00	0.75	1.00	1.00	1.00	1.00
1.00	1.00	1.00	1.00	1.00	1.00	1.00	1.00	1.00

Student B
Booklet taken = 5; Total scores = 32; Percentage correct responses = 76.19;
Item-response pattern (42 items)
111111011111010011111111100111100101011111
Attribute Mastery Probability (23 attributes)

1.00	1.00	1.00	1.00	1.00
0.60	1.00	0.64	1.00	1.00	1.00	0.79	1.00	1.00
1.00	1.00	1.00	1.00	1.00	1.00	1.00	1.00	0.21

Student C
Booklet taken = 3; Total scores = 38; Percentage correct responses = 90.48;
Item-response pattern (42 items)
111111011111111111111111001111110111111
Attribute Mastery Probability (23 attributes)

0.82	1.00	1.00	1.00	0.80
0.80	1.00	0.58	1.00	0.44	1.00	1.00	1.00	1.00
1.00	1.00	1.00	1.00	1.00	1.00	1.00	1.00	1.00

As shown in Figure 2, Student A, who answered around 90% of the test items correctly, had 20 perfect mastery attributes and only three attributes whose mastery probabilities were other than 1. These three attributes were data and basic statistics (C5), approximation and estimation (S4), and recognize patterns (S6). Thus, Student A had lower probabilities (below 0.80) of having mastered these three attributes.

Student B answered 76% of the items correctly and had 19 perfect mastery attributes and 4 attributes with lower mastery probabilities. These four attributes were number sense (S2), approximation and estimation (S4), novel/unfamiliar problems (S8), and quantitative reading (P10). Student B therefore had lower mastery probabilities for these four attributes, with a particularly low mastery probability for quantitative reading (P10; $P_{P10} = 0.21$), indicating he or she had a low likelihood of correctly answering items requiring this attribute.

On comparing Student C with Student A in Figure 2, we can see that both students obtained the same total score (38) in Booklet 3, which translated into their correctly answering about 90% of the items. However, the attribute mastery profile of Student C differed from that of Student A because of differences in the item-response patterns. Student C had five imperfect mastery attributes. Of these, the item-response patterns for data and basic statistics (C5), approximation and estimation (S4), and recognize patterns (S6) were imperfect, as was the case for Student A. Additionally, Student C had less than ideal response patterns for whole numbers and integers (C1) and number sense (S2). Furthermore, both students had somewhat different patterns of probability values on the imperfect mastery attributes.

Test Percentage Score Distribution for the Chinese Taipei Sample

Before summarizing the attribute mastery probabilities, we consider it useful to briefly mention the performance of the Chinese Taipei students on the TIMSS 1999 mathematics test. The box plot in Figure 3 shows that 25% of the students correctly answered 92% or more of the items, 50% of the students correctly answered 81% or more of the items, and 75% of the students correctly answered 62% or more of the items. In general, the distribution shows that Chinese Taipei students performed very well on the TIMSS 1999 mathematics items.

Descriptive Statistics of Attribute Mastery Probabilities

Table 3 presents the means and standard deviations of the mastery probabilities on the 23 attributes across the entire sample. As shown in the table, all attributes other than recognize patterns (S6) had mastery probabilities greater than 0.80. Fifteen of the 23 attributes had mean mastery probabilities above 0.90. This finding reflects the excellent performance of the Chinese Taipei students on the TIMSS 1999 mathematics tests, which is consistent with the fact that Chinese Taipei was the third highest performing country (according to scaled scores) of the 38 countries that participated in the study (Gonzalez & Miles, 2001). While it is useful to know how well the Chinese Taipei students fared, the information we obtained relative to the attribute mastery probabilities provides a more detailed examination of student learning than does the information provided by the scale scores.

Figure 3: Box plot of percentage of correct responses on the TIMSS 1999 mathematics test for Chinese Taipei students

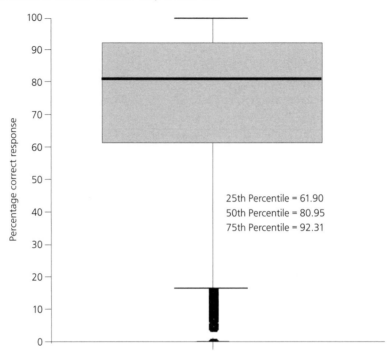

Among the five content attributes, Chinese Taipei students had the lowest mean probability on elementary algebra (C3) (P_{C3} = 0.88). They had the highest mean probabilities on whole numbers and integers (C1) (P_{C1} = 0.97) and fractions and decimals (C2) (P_{C2} = 0.98). In the skill/item-type attributes, the students performed very well on figures, tables, and graphs (S3), evaluate and verify options (S5), and word problems (S11), with mean probabilities of 0.99. For figures, tables, and graphs (S3) and word problems (S11), students had minimum mastery probabilities greater than 0 (P_{S3} = 0.20 and P_{S11} = 0.17, respectively). These findings mean that students who had the lowest overall performance still had approximately a 20% chance of mastering each of the two attributes. In addition, for recognize patterns (S6), two attributes had lower mean probabilities of 0.82. They were number sense (S2) and approximation and estimation (S4). The Chinese Taipei students performed particularly well on three process attributes: translate (P1) (P_{P1} = 0.98), computation application (P2) (P_{P2} = 0.98), and judgmental application (P3) (P_{P3} = 0.97). Lower achievement attributes were logical reasoning (P5) (P_{P5} = 0.84) and quantitative reading (P10) (P_{P10} = 0.83).

Using a mastery probability cut-off criterion of 0.85, we found that the Chinese Taipei students collectively mastered 18 of the 23 attributes and failed to master five. These non-mastered attributes included three skill attributes—number sense (S2), approximation and estimation (S4), and recognize patterns (S6)—as well as two process attributes—logical reasoning (P5) and quantitative reading (P10). The most

Table 3: Descriptive statistics of attribute probabilities for total sample (*N*=2,863)

Attribute		Mean[a]	SD	Minimum	Maximum
C1	Whole numbers and integers	0.97	0.11	0.00	1.00
C2	Fractions and decimals	0.98	0.11	0.00	1.00
C3	Elementary algebra	0.88	0.24	0.00	1.00
C4	Two-dimensional geometry	0.93	0.18	0.00	1.00
C5	Data and basic statistics	0.95	0.13	0.00	1.00
S2	Number sense	**0.82**	0.22	0.00	1.00
S3	Figures, tables, and graphs	0.99	0.05	0.20	1.00
S4	Approximation and estimation	**0.82**	0.19	0.00	1.00
S5	Evaluate and verify options	0.99	0.06	0.00	1.00
S6	Recognize patterns	**0.65**	0.29	0.00	1.00
S7	Proportional reasoning	0.97	0.12	0.00	1.00
S8	Novel/unfamiliar problems	0.92	0.17	0.00	1.00
S10	Open-ended items	0.87	0.26	0.00	1.00
S11	Word problems	0.99	0.06	0.17	1.00
P1	Translate	0.98	0.11	0.00	1.00
P2	Computation application	0.98	0.10	0.00	1.00
P3	Judgmental application	0.97	0.10	0.00	1.00
P4	Rule application in algebra	0.88	0.25	0.00	1.00
P5	Logical reasoning	**0.84**	0.29	0.00	1.00
P6	Solution search	0.92	0.18	0.00	1.00
P7	Visual figures and graphs	0.94	0.19	0.00	1.00
P9	Data management	0.94	0.17	0.00	1.00
P10	Quantitative reading	**0.83**	0.26	0.00	1.00

Note: [a] Mean mastery probabilities fall below cut-off of 0.85 for the attributes in bold type.

difficult attribute with the lowest probability of mastery for the students was recognize patterns (S6). In an earlier analysis, Tatsuoka and her colleagues (Tatsuoka, Corter, & Tatsuoka, 2004) found that recognize patterns was the most difficult attribute for students to master across the entire 20-country sample examined.

Although these numeric results are important, it is their interpretations in terms of students' skills that are of primary interest. According to Tatsuoka, Corter, and Guerrero's (2004) descriptions of cognitive attributes, recognize patterns (S6) is a skill that involves recognizing numeric, geometric, and/or algebraic patterns and finding a rule for generating those patterns. Within the realm of mathematics learning, this attribute can be viewed as an inductive thinking skill. Number sense (S2) is a skill that involves converting two or three different units into a comparable unit. In other words, the skill involves applying number properties and relationships. Approximation and estimation (S4) is a skill that requires the ability to estimate and approximate decimals or fractions in numbers, as well as in relation to areas or volumes in geometrical shapes. Logical reasoning (P5) includes case reasoning, deductive thinking skills, if–then, necessary and sufficient, and generalization skills. Quantitative and logical reading (P10) involves the ability to read and comprehend sentences containing mathematically quantitative terminology, such as "at least," "comparisons," "must be," and "increasing and decreasing," as well as logical quantifiers like "for every," "for any," and "for a given" (Tatsuoka, Corter, & Guerrero, 2004). These descriptions, and the results of the rule-space analyses with the Chinese Taipei sample, suggest that Chinese Taipei students are, in terms of the various mastery attributes, weakest in high-level mathematical thinking skills.

Clustered Knowledge States

The Cluster Analysis

This analysis specified solutions for 8 to 12 clusters. Table 4 presents the numbers of mastery attributes of the clustered knowledge states for each cluster solution. Because the goal of clustering is to explore educationally interpretable groups of students' attribute mastery probabilities and hierarchical relationships among these groups, we selected the 12-cluster solution as the final solution for the K-mean cluster analysis in this study. We considered other solutions, including 8- to 11-cluster solutions, but decided that these were not optimal. Our rationale for endorsing the 12-cluster solution follows.

First, some solutions did not yield the clustered knowledge state representing students who mastered all 23 attributes, such as the 9- and 10-cluster solutions (refer to Table 4). However, 325 students from the Chinese Taipei sample did master all attributes. In contrast, some solutions, such as the 8-cluster, did not yield the knowledge state reflecting students who mastered only a few attributes. Table 4 shows that the lowest numbers of clustered knowledge states in the eight-cluster solution were seven and eight attributes (except for 0 attributes). However, the clustered knowledge state characterized by four mastery attributes was evident in the 9-, 11-, and 12-cluster solutions. As for the 11-cluster solution, we were unable to derive interpretable hierarchical relationships among the clustered knowledge states. Essentially, interpretations for the 8- to 11-cluster solutions were problematic, while the 12-cluster solution yielded the clustered knowledge states that not only reflected students' attribute performances at different achievement levels, but also supported interpretable hierarchical relationships among them. Further statistical evidence is provided below to support our claim that the 12-cluster solution allowed apportionment of attribute masteries to separate distinct clusters.

Table 4: Number of mastered attributes associated with each of the clustered knowledge states for different cluster solutions

Knowledge state	Solution				
	8-cluster	9-cluster	10-cluster	11-cluster	12-cluster
KS 1	18	0	8	19	17
KS 2	18	18	12	16	1
KS 3	13	21	0	10	11
KS 4	23	9	17	10	0
KS 5	8	14	18	4	4
KS 6	21	4	7	23	19
KS 7	7	18	21	18	23
KS 8	0	18	18	13	13
KS 9		10	9	0	22
KS 10			22	19	18
KS 11				21	12
KS 12					21

We labeled the 12 clusters KS1 to KS12. The average distance between the students and their classified cluster centroids was 0.51 and ranged from 0 to 1.62. The distance values from cluster centroids were also quite small, thereby indicating that, with the 12-cluster solution, the classified students were representative of their clusters. In addition, the numbers of students in 10 of the clusters for the 12-cluster solution were substantial, with each cluster containing more than 1% of the total sample (> 30 students). Exceptions were the clusters for KS2 and KS4 (three students and one student, respectively). KS2 and KS4 represented students with low mastery probabilities on all or almost all of the attributes. Few students were classified into KS2 and KS4 because of the high mathematics achievement overall of the Chinese Taipei students. These two are cognitively and educationally interpretable knowledge states in terms of the hierarchical relationships shown in Figure 4. These reasons led us to apply, in this study, the 12-cluster solution that included KS2 and KS4.

We also used univariate analysis of variance (ANOVA) on each attribute in order to understand how important each was in separating out the groups in the 12-clustered solution. The results on each attribute for the 12-cluster solution appear in Table 5. However, these results, especially the F values, serve only as guidelines for descriptive purposes because the K-mean cluster analysis maximized the differences among the cases in the different clusters. The results in Table 5 show that the F values were far from 1.0 and quite large; thus, by using the 12-cluster solution, we were able to show that every attribute was useful for separating clusters. Accordingly, we agreed that the 12-cluster solution was a cognitively interpretable solution in this study.

Figure 4: A hierarchically ordered network among the clustered knowledge states

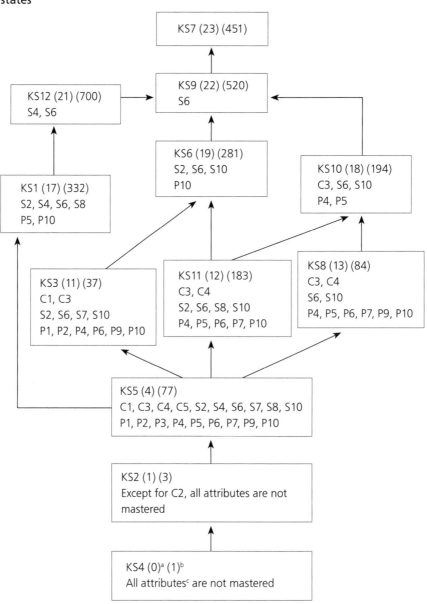

Notes:

[a] The first number in parenthesis represents the number of mastery attributes.

[b] The second number in parenthesis represents sample size.

[c] Attributes presented in the rectangles were not mastered.

Table 5: One-way ANOVA results evaluating differences across the 12 knowledge states for each attribute

		Attribute	Cluster	Error
		Mean square $(df = 11)$	Mean square $(df = 2851)$	F
C1	Whole numbers and integers	1.162	0.007	175.786
C2	Fractions and decimals	0.391	0.011	35.502
C3	Elementary algebra	9.714	0.018	532.022
C4	Two-dimensional geometry	3.652	0.020	181.231
C5	Data and basic statistics	0.842	0.014	59.642
S2	Number sense	4.073	0.033	123.826
S3	Figures, tables, and graphs	0.120	0.002	58.944
S4	Approximation and estimation	3.751	0.022	167.813
S5	Evaluate and verify options	0.199	0.002	86.830
S6	Recognize patterns	15.578	0.026	607.143
S7	Proportional reasoning	1.537	0.010	157.827
S8	Novel/unfamiliar problems	1.835	0.021	88.816
S10	Open-ended items	9.438	0.033	289.037
S11	Word problems	0.136	0.003	40.905
P1	Translate	1.287	0.006	202.054
P2	Computation application	0.773	0.008	100.606
P3	Judgmental application	0.360	0.009	38.004
P4	Rule application in algebra	11.263	0.019	577.865
P5	Logical reasoning	11.367	0.040	284.532
P6	Solution search	3.193	0.019	171.370
P7	Visual figures and graphs	5.468	0.014	387.972
P9	Data management	1.645	0.023	73.051
P10	Quantitative reading	9.347	0.030	313.577

Note: $p < 0.001$ for all attributes.

Description for the Clustered Knowledge States

Table 6 presents the means (centroids) of the mastery probabilities of the 23 attributes for each of the 12 clustered knowledge states across the students classified into each group. The mean probabilities across the 23 attributes and the sample sizes for each of the 12 clustered knowledge states appear at the bottom of Table 6. By applying the cut-off of 0.85, we were able to transform the vectors of the mean mastery probabilities for the 12 clustered knowledge states into binary indictor vectors, thereby forming attribute mastery patterns for each of the 12 clustered knowledge states. These are shown in Table 7.

The attribute mastery patterns corresponding to the knowledge states presented in Table 7 facilitate interpretation of the cluster-analysis results in Table 6. Here, we computed the total numbers of mastery attributes for the clustered knowledge states and then sorted the knowledge states by the descending order of the total number from the left-most to the right-most columns. Table 7 therefore also presents the mean mastery probabilities and sample sizes adopted from Table 6 for the 12-cluster solution of knowledge states.

As is evident in Table 7, knowledge states KS7, KS9, and KS12 had the highest mean mastery probabilities with 0.98, 0.96, and 0.96, respectively. These three knowledge states not only corresponded to the binary indicator vectors for mastery attributes but also had the highest numbers of mastery attributes. KS7 was represented by all 23 mastery attributes. KS9 consisted of 22 mastery attributes and one non-mastery attribute, namely, recognize patterns (S6). KS12 comprised 21 mastery attributes and two non-mastery attributes—recognize patterns (S6) and approximation and estimation (S4)—which were the most difficult attributes for the students to master. Because these three knowledge states had the highest mastery probabilities and included the largest numbers of mastery attributes, it was possible to categorize them into the highest level of performance knowledge states for the Chinese Taipei sample. The students classified into these three knowledge states failed to master only two (at most) of the 23 attributes. Approximately 58% of the students (i.e., 1,671 students out of the total sample of 2,863) "classified" into this highest level of performance knowledge state.

KS1, KS6, and KS10 had mean mastery probabilities of 0.91, 0.88, and 0.87, respectively. These three can therefore be thought of as the second highest level of performance knowledge state for the Chinese Taipei students because their mean mastery probabilities of knowledge states were still greater than 0.85, which was a criterion for individual attribute mastery. Approximately 28% of the students (i.e., 807 out of 2,863) fell within this second highest level of performance knowledge state. In sum, 86% of Chinese Taipei students fell within the top two levels of knowledge states.

KS3, KS8, and KS11 had mean mastery probabilities of 0.70, 0.76, and 0.79, respectively. The corresponding numbers of mastery attributes were 11, 13, and 12. Interestingly, more process attributes than other attributes were not mastered in these three knowledge states. Given that KS3, KS8, and KS11 had around half of all 23 attributes mastered, we categorized these three knowledge states into the middle level of performance. Approximately 11% of the students (304 out of 2,863) classified into these mid-level performance knowledge states.

Finally, KS5, KS2, and KS4 had the lowest mean mastery probabilities of 0.68, 0.46, and 0.17, respectively. KS5 had four attributes mastered, while KS2 had only one. KS4 had no attributes mastered. The mastery attributes in KS5 comprised fractions and decimals (C2), figures, tables, and graphs (S3), evaluate and verify options (S5), and word problems (S11). These mastery attributes in KS5 were the easiest attributes

Table 6: Centroids of the clustered knowledge states

Attribute		Knowledge states											
		1	2	3	4	5	6	7	8	9	10	11	12
C1	Whole numbers and integers	1	0.27	0.77	0.20	0.67	0.94	1	0.89	0.99	0.97	0.97	1
C2	Fractions and decimals	0.98	1	0.86	0.00	0.89	0.98	1	0.97	1	0.97	0.89	1
C3	Elementary algebra	0.96	0.07	0.21	0.00	0.51	0.94	0.99	0.72	0.99	0.54	0.47	0.98
C4	Two-dimensional geometry	0.93	0.20	0.93	0.00	0.66	0.97	0.97	0.46	1	0.91	0.71	0.97
C5	Data and basic statistics	0.99	0.20	0.95	0.20	0.72	0.88	0.99	0.94	0.95	0.93	0.98	0.96
S2	Number sense	0.60	0.60	0.76	0.00	0.58	0.74	0.97	0.90	0.91	0.89	0.65	0.85
S3	Figures, tables, and graphs	1	0.67	1	0.40	0.91	0.99	1	0.98	1	0.99	0.98	1
S4	Approximation and estimation	0.77	0.73	0.89	0.00	0.74	0.87	0.98	0.87	0.90	0.87	0.86	0.64
S5	Evaluate and verify options	1	0.53	0.96	0.20	0.89	0.99	1	0.98	1	0.99	1	1
S6	Recognize patterns	0.83	0.00	0.18	0.00	0.19	0.24	0.98	0.33	0.53	0.72	0.39	0.78
S7	Proportional reasoning	0.97	0.73	0.37	0.40	0.80	0.98	0.98	0.97	0.99	0.94	0.99	0.99
S8	Novel/unfamiliar problems	0.73	0.73	0.85	0.60	0.81	0.94	0.96	0.96	0.98	0.92	0.81	0.98
S10	Open-ended items	0.97	0.07	0.47	0.00	0.46	0.63	0.99	0.49	0.97	0.81	0.49	1
S11	Word problems	1	0.67	0.95	0.40	0.90	0.99	1	0.99	1	0.98	0.98	1
P1	Translate	0.99	0.40	0.48	0.20	0.79	0.99	0.99	1	1	0.95	0.98	1
P2	Computation application	0.99	0.80	0.84	0.00	0.70	0.99	0.99	0.98	1	0.96	0.97	1
P3	Judgmental application	0.99	0.67	0.86	0.20	0.83	0.98	0.99	0.96	0.99	0.95	0.92	0.98
P4	Rule application in algebra	0.97	0.13	0.18	0.00	0.41	0.96	0.97	0.59	0.97	0.42	0.59	1
P5	Logical reasoning	0.69	0.47	0.86	0.60	0.68	0.90	0.96	0.26	0.95	0.79	0.27	0.98
P6	Solution search	0.97	0.53	0.30	0.20	0.59	0.88	0.99	0.78	0.95	0.88	0.79	0.98
P7	Visual figures and graphs	0.98	0.67	0.93	0.00	0.72	0.93	0.99	0.19	1	0.94	0.83	1
P9	Data management	0.94	0.20	0.78	0.00	0.59	0.95	0.96	0.77	0.98	0.90	0.91	0.99
P10	Quantitative reading	0.58	0.33	0.76	0.20	0.59	0.50	0.98	0.43	0.95	0.87	0.77	0.97
Mean		0.91	0.46	0.70	0.17	0.68	0.88	0.98	0.76	0.96	0.87	0.79	0.96
Sample size		332	3	37	1	77	281	451	84	520	194	183	700

for the entire Chinese Taipei sample. It was therefore possible to categorize KS5, KS2, and KS4 into the low level of performance because students mastered so few of their attributes. Only 3% (81 out of 2,863) of the students fell within this level of performance. The mean mastery probability across 23 attributes for each of the middle- and low-level performing knowledge states was below the 0.85 criterion. Thus, only

Table 7: Order attribute mastery patterns for the clustered knowledge states

Attribute		Knowledge states											
		7	9	12	6	10	1	8	11	3	5	2	4
C1	Whole numbers and integers	1	1	1	1	1	1	1	1	0	0	0	0
C2	Fractions and decimals	1	1	1	1	1	1	1	1	1	1	1	0
C3	Elementary algebra	1	1	1	1	0	1	0	0	0	0	0	0
C4	Two-dimensional geometry	1	1	1	1	1	1	0	0	1	0	0	0
C5	Data and basic statistics	1	1	1	1	1	1	1	1	1	0	0	0
S2	Number sense	1	1	1	0	1	0	1	0	0	0	0	0
S3	Figures, tables, and graphs	1	1	1	1	1	1	1	1	1	1	0	0
S4	Approximation and estimation	1	1	0	1	1	0	1	1	1	0	0	0
S5	Evaluate and verify options	1	1	1	1	1	1	1	1	1	1	0	0
S6	Recognize patterns	1	0	0	0	0	0	0	0	0	0	0	0
S7	Proportional reasoning	1	1	1	1	1	1	1	1	0	0	0	0
S8	Novel/unfamiliar problems	1	1	1	1	1	0	1	0	1	0	0	0
S10	Open-ended items	1	1	1	0	0	1	0	0	0	0	0	0
S11	Word problems	1	1	1	1	1	1	1	1	1	1	0	0
P1	Translate	1	1	1	1	1	1	1	1	0	0	0	0
P2	Computation application	1	1	1	1	1	1	1	1	0	0	0	0
P3	Judgmental application	1	1	1	1	1	1	1	1	1	0	0	0
P4	Rule application in algebra	1	1	1	1	0	1	0	0	0	0	0	0
P5	Logical reasoning	1	1	1	1	0	0	0	0	1	0	0	0
P6	Solution search	1	1	1	1	1	1	0	0	0	0	0	0
P7	Visual figures and graphs	1	1	1	1	1	1	0	0	1	0	0	0
P9	Data management	1	1	1	1	1	1	0	1	0	0	0	0
P10	Quantitative reading	1	1	1	0	1	0	0	0	0	0	0	0
Number of mastery attributes		23	22	21	19	18	17	13	12	11	4	1	0
Mean of mastery probability		0.98	0.96	0.96	0.88	0.87	0.91	0.76	0.79	0.70	0.68	0.46	0.17
Sample size		451	520	700	281	194	332	84	183	37	77	3	1

Note: The cut-off point for mastery probability was set at 0.85.

14% of the Chinese Taipei students fell into these two lowest-level knowledge states.

A Hierarchically-ordered Network

Our analysis also involved applying the principles of inclusion relations and graph theory to establish the hierarchical relationships and the network existing among the knowledge states. As seen in Table 7, knowledge state 7 (KS7) had a hierarchical relationship with knowledge state 9 (KS9) because each component in the binary mastery vector of KS7 was larger than or equal to the relative component in the mastery vector of KS9. Figure 4 presents a hierarchically ordered network that depicts the various relationships among these 12 clustered knowledge states. The knowledge states with few mastered attributes, such as KS2 and KS4, were located in the lower portion of the network. In contrast, the knowledge states with more mastered attributes, such as KS7 and KS9, were located in the upper portion of the network.

DISCUSSION AND CONCLUSIONS

Implications of the Results

The empirical study presented in this paper involved a substantive examination of the mathematics achievement of Chinese Taipei Grade 8 students who participated in TIMSS 1999 (TIMSS-R). We applied rule-space methodology (RSM) to produce a diagnostic description of these students' cognitive abilities and skills as related to the TIMSS items. RSM employed within the auspices of a well-designed cognitive model successfully provided diagnostic information for the Chinese Taipei sample, and in so doing confirmed, as have other studies, that RSM is a viable alternative to traditional psychometric analysis of test scores.

In the TIMSS 1999 survey, Chinese Taipei ranked third among the 38 participating countries, based on the first plausible values on the mathematics test. Thus, in terms of an overall estimate of student ability across countries, Chinese Taipei students proved to be among the most able. The reproduction of these results with RSM supports the usefulness of this method for providing diagnostic information that augments overall score estimates with descriptions of cognitive attributes for a particular population of interest. Note, however, that RSM cannot provide diagnostic information relating to attribute mastery probabilities for students who have not been successfully classified into one of the predetermined knowledge states. If methods such as rule-space were implemented for score reporting, then handling of score reports for students not classified into a diagnostic group would need to be considered carefully. The best way to avoid this situation is to develop a complete and accurate Q-matrix that accounts for the skills underlying test performance. In situations where there are many unclassified students, the components of the proposed cognitive models (e.g., the list of attributes and the Q-matrix) would need to be revisited. By checking the item-response patterns of unclassified students, researchers conducting the analysis should be able to find new attributes from which they can create a new cognitive model for the test.

In general, the Chinese Taipei students performed well on all cognitive attributes other than recognize patterns, and their excellent performance was evident in the distributions of the 12 clustered knowledge states. The students also showed some weaknesses on thinking skills (inductive and deductive reasoning) and algebra content, compared with the other mastery attributes. These findings suggest that the teaching practices associated with mathematics in classrooms in Chinese Taipei middle schools may be having an effect. As in other Asian countries, such as Japan, South Korea, Singapore, and Hong Kong (SAR), Chinese Taipei students in middle and high schools study within a highly academic and peer-competitive learning environment. The foremost task of middle and high school teachers in Chinese Taipei is to help students acquire high scores on entrance examinations so that students can gain admission from high schools into colleges and universities. Hence, much instruction is examination-oriented. Teachers in these educational environments tend to emphasize memorization and repeated practice as important elements in students' learning, including mathematics learning (Leung, 2001; Liu, 1986).

Mathematics teachers in Chinese Taipei have sufficient and diverse mathematics knowledge because they have to pass the rigorous college entrance examination and take mathematics-related courses amounting to 80 credits in their colleges (Saul, 2000). As such, they are generally knowledgeable about the topics they teach and are able to provide students with diverse ways to solve mathematical questions. However, the lecture approach is still a prevalent pedagogy in mathematics classrooms in Chinese Taipei. Under this approach, students seldom have opportunity to ask questions. Their major task is to listen carefully to what the mathematics teachers teach, and to show their motivation by concentrating on mathematics learning through practice and repetition (Saul, 2000). Mathematics teachers also frequently assign homework to help students apply mathematics concepts and become more familiar with content knowledge. After class, most students go to enrichment programs or have private tutors to review what they have learned in schools and to teach them effective test-taking strategies. At home, students work hard on homework and repeatedly practice using supplemental materials. Given these instructional techniques, it is not surprising that Chinese Taipei students perform well not only on TIMSS but also on other studies of international mathematics achievement.

However, an overemphasis on mathematics examinations can result in the pursuit of correct answers rather than in a true understanding of mathematics. Students may use the right solutions to solve the test items, but they may or may not know why the solutions are appropriate for the questions. The current mathematics learning processes appear to lead to Chinese Taipei students not receiving instruction that encourages individual thinking skills. Instead, they are encouraged to spend time becoming familiar with test item solutions as taught by their mathematics teachers rather than developing their own solutions. These teaching practices may, in part, explain why Chinese Taipei students are somewhat weaker in mathematical thinking and reasoning skills relative to their performance on the other mastery cognitive attributes.

The hypothesized relationship between instructional style and skills mastery can be further highlighted by considering earlier research from other countries. For example, RSM results for Japan, another country that performed extremely well on TIMSS 1999, show that the Japanese students achieved this result because they had excellent high-level thinking skills. In particular, Japanese students performed well on logical reasoning (P5), solution search (P6), judgmental application (P3), data management (P9), and recognize patterns (S6) (Tatsuoka, Corter, & Tatsuoka, 2004). Tatsuoka and her colleagues hypothesized that this result may be a product of the mathematics teaching practices evident in Japanese classrooms. Their review of Kawanaka and

Stigler's (1999) study regarding TIMSS video data of classroom practices showed that Japanese teachers encourage students to develop divergent solutions to problems instead of simply lecturing them on mathematical content knowledge and explaining how to solve problems in classrooms. In other words, teachers in Japan emphasize developing students' mathematical thinking skills rather than having students simply solve problems. It seems, then, that instructional strategies that develop particular cognitive skills advantage students' mathematics achievement. Accordingly, Chinese Taipei mathematics teachers may want to consider providing students with more time to develop their thinking regarding mathematical questions and content.

Singapore provides another example in support of this claim. Students in this country also gained high mean scores on the TIMSS 1999 mathematics test. Moreover, Singapore has an educational context similar to that of Chinese Taipei. Birenbaum, Tatsuoka, and Xin (2005) conducted a study to compare the mathematics performance of students in the United States, Singapore, and Israel. They explored various aspects of the educational context of Singapore and concluded that Singapore has a strong examination culture. Parents support their children's education, particularly in terms of encouraging them to prepare for examinations. Singapore's teachers also focus on helping students prepare for the frequent examinations, and they set time aside for instruction directed at increasing students' test-taking abilities. The teachers also tend to emphasize rote memorization. Children spend a lot of time after class studying mathematics. As Tatsuoka, Corter, & Tatsuoka (2004) found, Singapore's high scores on mathematics resulted from students' excellence in computational and reading skills rather than from their high-level thinking skills. This finding aligns strongly with the findings of the current study. This consistent relationship between the type of instruction and skill mastery is useful and promising because it provides evidence of how instructional strategies affect students' learning in terms of the type of cognitive skills those strategies encourage.

In summary, within Chinese Taipei, strong emphases on memorizing lessons and repeated practice appear to lead to overall high achievement in mathematics. However, this approach may limit development of specific high-level thinking skills among students. Although Chinese Taipei students achieve excellence with respect to total mathematics scores as well as many cognitive attributes related to mathematics, the Chinese Taipei government could consider ways to improve relative weaknesses in the mathematics curriculum, in pedagogical approaches, and in mathematics teacher education. Models such as those employed by the Singaporean educational authorities that promote, despite students' existing high levels of achievement, the need for students to continue acquiring the competencies underpinning a successful economy (Birenbaum et al., 2005) could provide a template for modifications to Chinese Taipei mathematics instruction.

SUGGESTIONS AND RECOMMENDATIONS

The findings from this study bring forth several suggestions for further research relating to cognitive diagnostic assessment. One suggestion relates directly to the rule-space method in terms of the cut-off point of probability for attribute mastery. Different cut-off values affect the outputs of rule-space analysis, such as the hierarchical relationships among the knowledge states. In order to make these hierarchical relations most reliable, it is very important to determine an optimal cut-off score. How this might be done within the context of rule-space analyses is a crucial and interesting topic for future research.

Alternative methods of analyzing the information gained from RSM may improve our understanding of student proficiencies and skills. By using the new attribute probability dataset, researchers should be able to conduct statistical analyses that make rule-space results more interpretable and meaningful. For example, they could apply factor analysis to explore attributes with common underlying factors. The results of such an analysis should allow precise definition of the strengths and weaknesses of student performance on mathematics tests as well as comparisons of groups of students. These analyses could also be improved through use of multilevel models and/or hierarchical linear models. These complex models could allow for analysis of cognitive attributes alongside consideration of educational context variables, such as teaching strategies, teacher characteristics, and school context variables (see, for example Xin, Xu, & Tatsuoka, 2004, in this regard). Additional studies utilizing a multilevel approach may provide useful information for researchers and practitioners interested in the contextual and environmental factors that affect students' mathematics achievement.

Overall, RSM can be used to provide diagnostic information relative to cognitive skills and thereby enrich interpretations of test scores by and for students, teachers, and administrators. Ultimately, continued development of RSM and statistical methods for analyzing the resulting information should help improve the interpretability of assessment results and lead to more widespread application of RSM in the future.

References

Birenbaum, M., Kelly, A. E., & Tatsuoka, K. K. (1993). Diagnosing knowledge states in algebra using the rule-space model. *Journal of Research in Mathematics Education, 24*, 442–459.

Birenbaum, M., Tatsuoka, C., & Xin, T. (2005). Large-scale diagnostic assessment: Comparison of eighth graders' mathematics performance in the United States, Singapore and Israel. *Assessment in Education, 12*, 167–181.

Chen, Y.-H., Gorin, J. S., Thompson, M. S., & Tatsuoka, K. K. (2008). Cross-cultural validity of the TIMSS-1999 mathematics test: Verification of a cognitive model. *The International Journal of Testing, 8*, 251–271.

Corter, J. E., & Tatsuoka, K. K. (2002). *Cognitive and measurement foundations of diagnostic assessments in mathematics* (College Board technical report). New York: Teachers College, Columbia University.

Embretson, S. E. (1984). A general latent trait model for response processes. *Psychometrika, 49*, 175–186.

Embretson, S. E. (Ed.). (1985). *Test design: Developments in psychology and psychometrics* (pp. 195–218). Orlando, FL: Academic Press.

Embretson, S. E. (1993). Psychometric models for learning and cognitive processes. In N. Frederiksen, R. J. Mislevy, & I. I. Bejar (Eds.), *Test theory for a new generation of tests* (pp. 125–150). Hillsdale, NJ: Lawrence Erlbaum Associates.

Embretson, S. E., & Gorin, J. S. (2001). Improving construct validity with cognitive psychology principles. *Journal of Educational Measurement, 38*, 343–368.

Embretson, S. E., & Reise, S. P. (2000). *Item response theory for psychologists.* Mahwah, NJ: Lawrence Erlbaum Associates.

Everson, H. T., Guerrero, A., & Yamada, T. (2003). *Understanding group differences in mathematical knowledge states: A rule-space analysis of the black-white correlates of mathematical reasoning.* Paper presented at the annual meeting of the National Council of Measurement in Education (NCME), Chicago, Illinois.

Fischer, G. H. (1973). Linear logistic test model as an instrument in educational research. *Acta Psychologica, 37*, 359–374.

Gonzalez, E. J., & Miles, J. A. (2001). *TIMSS 1999 user guide for the international database: IEA's repeat of the Third International Mathematics and Science Study at the eighth grade.* Chestnut Hill, MA: Boston College.

Gorin, J. S. (2002). *Cognitive and psychometric modeling of text-based reading-comprehension GRE-V items.* Unpublished doctoral dissertation, University of Kansas.

Herman, J. J. (1991). Research in cognition and learning: Implications for achievement testing practice. In M. C. Wittrock & E. L. Baker (Eds.), *Testing and cognition* (pp. 154–165). Englewood Cliffs, NJ: Prentice Hall.

Kawanaka, T., & Stigler, J. W. (1999). Teachers' use of questions in eighth-grade mathematics classrooms in Germany, Japan, and the United States. *Mathematical Thinking and Learning, 1*, 255–278.

Leung, F. K. S. (2001). In search of an East Asian identity in mathematics education. *Educational Studies in Mathematics, 47*, 35–51.

Linn, R. L. (1989). *Has item response theory increased the validity of achievement test scores?* (CSE technical report 302). Los Angeles, CA: UCLA Center for Research on Evaluation, Standards, and Student Testing.

Liu, I. M. (1986). Chinese cognition. In M. N. Bond (Ed.), *The psychology of the Chinese people* (pp. 73–105). Hong Kong: Oxford University Press.

Mislevy, R. J. (1994). Evidence and inference in educational assessment. *Psychometrika, 60*, 439–483.

Mullis, I. V. S., Martin, M. O., Gonzalez, E. J., Gregory, K. D., Garden R. A., O'Connor, K. M., Chrostowski, S. J., & Smith, T. A. (2000). *TIMSS 1999 international mathematics report: Findings from IEA's repeat of the Third International Mathematics and Science Study at the eighth grade*. Chestnut Hill, MA: Boston College.

Saul, M. (2000). Reifying the research: Mathematics education in Taiwan. *Notices of the AMS, 47*, 360–363.

Snow, R. E., & Lohman, D. F. (1989). Implications of cognitive psychology for educational measurement. In R. L. Linn (Ed.), *Educational measurement* (pp. 263–331). New York: Macmillan.

Stout, W. (2002). Psychometrics: From practice to theory and back. *Psychometrika, 67*, 485–518.

Tatsuoka, C., Varadi, F., & Tatsuoka, K. K. (1992). *BUGSHELL* (computer software). Ewing, NJ: Tanar Software.

Tatsuoka, K. K. (1983). Rule space: An approach for dealing with misconceptions based on item response theory. *Journal of Educational Measurement, 20*, 345–354.

Tatsuoka, K. K. (1984). Caution indices based on item response theory. *Psychometrika, 49*, 95–110.

Tatsuoka, K. K. (1990). Toward an integration of item-response theory and cognitive error diagnosis. In N. Grederiksen, R. Glazer, A. Lesgold, & M. G. Shafto (Eds.), *Diagnostic monitoring of skill and knowledge acquisition* (pp. 453–488). Hillsdale, NJ: Lawrence Erlbaum Associates.

Tatsuoka, K. K. (1991). *Boolean algebra applied to determination of the universal set of knowledge states* (technical report ONR-91-1). Princeton, NJ: Educational Testing Service.

Tatsuoka, K. K. (1995). Architecture of knowledge structures and cognitive diagnosis: A statistical pattern recognition and classification approach. In P. D. Nichols, S. F. Chipman, & R. L. Brennan (Eds.), *Cognitively diagnostic assessment* (pp. 327–359). Hillsdale, NJ: Lawrence Erlbaum Associates.

Tatsuoka, K. K. (1996). Use of generalized person-fit indices: Zetas for statistical pattern classification. *Applied Measurement in Education, 9*, 65–75.

Tatsuoka, K. K., & Boodoo, G. (2000). Subgroup differences on the GRE quantitative test based on the underlying cognitive processes and knowledge. In A. E. Kelly & R. Lesh (Eds.), *Handbook of research design in mathematics and science education* (pp. 821–857). Hillsdale, NJ: Erlbaum.

Tatsuoka, K. K., Corter, J. E., & Guerrero, A. (2004). *Coding manual for identifying involvement of content, skill, and process subskills for the TIMSS-R 8th grade and 12th grade general mathematics test items* (technical report). New York: Department of Human Development, Teachers College, Columbia University.

Tatsuoka, K. K., Corter, J. E., & Tatsuoka, C. (2004). Patterns of diagnosed mathematical content and process skills in TIMSS-R across a sample of 20 countries. *American Educational Research Journal, 41*, 901–926.

Tatsuoka, K. K., Guerrero, A., Corter, J. E., Yamada, T., & Tatsuoka, C. (2003). *International comparisons of mathematical thinking skills in the TIMSS-R*. Paper presented at the annual meeting of the National Council of Measurement in Education (NCME), Chicago, Illinois.

Tatsuoka, K. K., & Tatsuoka, M. M. (1987). Bug distribution and statistical pattern classification. *Psychometrika, 52*, 193–206.

Tatsuoka, K. K., Xin, T., Corter, J. E., & Tatsuoka, C. (2004). *Patterns of attribute characteristic curves and their relationships to teachers' background variables*. Paper presented at the annual meeting of the National Council of Measurement in Education (NCME), San Diego, California.

Xin, T., Xu, Z., & Tatsuoka, K. K. (2004). Linkage between teacher quality, student achievement, and cognitive skills: A rule-space model. *Studies in Educational Evaluation, 30*, 205–223.

Estimation of a Rasch model including subdimensions

Steffen Brandt
Leibniz Institute for Science Education, Kiel, Germany

Many achievement tests, particularly in large-scale assessments, deal with measuring abilities that are themselves assumed to be composed of other more specific abilities. A common approach to obtaining all necessary ability estimates, therefore, is to analyze the same data once using a unidimensional model and once using a multidimensional model. This approach not only poses a theoretical contradiction but also means neglecting the assumed local dependencies between the items of the same "specific" ability within the unidimensional model. This paper presents the application of a Rasch subdimension model that explicitly considers local item dependence (LID) due to specific abilities and thereby yields more adequate estimates. In addition to providing a short theoretical presentation of the model, the paper focuses on making it easier for researchers to apply the model. The paper accordingly uses an empirical example to show how results using the subdimension model differ from results arising out of the unidimensional model, the multidimensional model, and the Rasch testlet model (as an alternative model that models LID). It also offers an explicit description of how ConQuest software can be used to define and calibrate the models.

INTRODUCTION

Many of today's achievement tests, in particular those used within large-scale assessments, deal with measuring abilities that are themselves assumed to be composed of other more specific abilities. As such, a common approach that researchers involved in large-scale cross-national assessments such as TIMSS and PISA take when endeavoring to yield the necessary ability estimates is to analyze the same data-set once using a unidimensional model and once using a multidimensional model (cf. Martin, Mullis, & Chrostowski, 2004; Organisation for Economic Co-operation and Development/OECD, 2005). However, this approach has two major downsides. First, from a theoretical point of view, the assumption that the data fit both unidimensional and multidimensional models seems to make model-fit tests obsolete and the application of a particular model somewhat arbitrary—or simply determined by pragmatic needs. Second, and this time from a practical point of view, neglecting the assumed local dependencies among the items of the same subtest (or subdimension) that measure a more specific ability means accepting the negative impacts of local item dependence (LID).

As shown by many authors (Sireci, Thissen, & Wainer, 1991; Thissen, Steinberg, & Mooney, 1989; Wang & Wilson, 2005a; Yen, 1993), an inappropriate assumption of LID results in an overestimation of test information and reliability and an underestimation of the measurement error. Furthermore, because LID influences item discriminations, items showing LID also show lower discriminations than is the case with items showing no LID (Yen, 1993). Finally, the variance of the estimated parameters decreases for items with LID.

Yen and Thissen and his colleagues have examined these effects of LID through the use of "testlets"—a subset of items in a test that have a common structural element. An example is bundles that have a common stimulus (Wainer & Kiely, 1987). More recently, Wang and Wilson (2005a, 2005b) showed that it is possible to model LID in relation to testlets by using a Rasch testlet model and thereby obtaining more precise and adequate estimates. The Rasch testlet and the Rasch subdimension model proposed below are special cases of the group of so-called bi-factor models. These models are characterized by the fact that each item loads on at least two dimensions, on a general factor, and on one or more group—or method-specific—factors, such that the loading on the general factor is non-zero (Holzinger & Swineford, 1937).

In order to analyze these types of models, Gibbons and Hedeker (1992) developed a full-information item bi-factor analysis for binary item responses. The development of appropriate models and estimation procedures relative to graded response data has, however, been less successful (cf. Muraki & Carlson, 1995). The additional computational complexity associated with graded response data leads to the introduction of additional model constraints in order to estimate the model. One restriction commonly applied involves constraining the method-specific—or group-specific—factors (denoted in the case of the model presented in the following section as the latent traits of the *subdimensions*) so that the factors are independent from the general factor (termed the "main dimension" in the following). While this constraint is appropriate in that the specific factors measure only the residual associations of the items beyond those due to the general latent trait, and although this constraint is a common feature of bi-factor models, the computational complexity seems to make a second model constraint necessary for graded response data. As a consequence, an additional assumption in regard to the Rasch testlet model, as well as in regard to the recently proposed full-information item bi-factor analysis for graded response data (Gibbons et al., 2007), is that the specific factors are also independent of one another.

The model that I propose in this paper tries to loosen this latter—rather strong—constraint through application of a different constraint but one that still allows for correlation of the specific factors. I discuss the possible consequences of these different assumptions in somewhat more detail after defining the model in the next section. I then show how to calibrate the model using the software ConQuest. This is followed by an empirical example that depicts the differences between the unidimensional, the (unrestricted) multidimensional, and the subdimension models.

A RASCH MODEL THAT INCLUDES SUBDIMENSIONS

To resolve the theoretical problem of unidimensionality versus multidimensionality and to reduce negative impacts on measurement precision due to LID, the model proposed here is a Rasch subdimension model (Brandt, 2007a, 2008b). The model extends the standard Rasch model (Rasch, 1980) by using an additional set of parameters for subdimensions, and it is based on the assumption that each person has a general ability in the measured dimension (which in the subdimension model is denoted as the *main* dimension) as well as strengths and weaknesses (to be defined *ex ante*) in the subdimensions that measure specific abilities within the measured main dimension. This way, the model is able to yield person parameters that account for existing LID among the items of the same subdimension. The model is also a special case of the multidimensional random coefficients multinomial logit model (MRCMLM) (Adams, Wilson, & Wang, 1997), and so can be directly estimated through use of the software ConQuest (Wu, Adams, & Wilson, 1998).

Model Definition

Assuming we have a single measured main dimension (e.g., mathematics) that is composed of a number of defined subdimensions (e.g., differently defined areas of mathematics), and assuming that we can characterize each person's ability in a subdimension according to a strength or weakness relative to his or her ability in the measured main dimension, we end up with three different sorts of parameters to consider when modeling the answers based on a Rasch model approach. The first two sorts of parameters are analogous to the Rasch model, the item parameters b_i (with $i=1,...,I$ and I the total number of items) that describe the item difficulties, and the person parameters θ_v (with $v=1,...,V$ and V the total number of persons) that describe persons' abilities on the measured main dimension. In addition to these parameters, we need parameters γ_{vd} that describe persons' strengths (or weaknesses) in the measured subdimensions. A person's actual ability parameter to solve an item from subdimension d (with $d=1,...,D$ and D the total number of subdimensions) is thus defined by

$$\theta_{vd} = \theta_v + \gamma_{vd}.$$ (1)

While the parameter θ_v denotes the *overall* ability parameter across subdimensions, the parameter γ_{vd} denotes the *specific* ability parameter for the subdimension. If we use the definition in Equation (1), the probability P_{vi1} of person v producing a correct response to a dichotomous item i in a Rasch subdimension model is then given as

$$P_{vi1} = \frac{\exp\left(\theta_v + \gamma_{vd(i)} - b_i\right)}{1 + \exp\left(\theta_v + \gamma_{vd(i)} - b_i\right)}$$ (2)

where $\gamma_{vd(i)} = d(i) \cdot \gamma_{vd}$ and $d(i)$ is equal to 1 when item i measures subdimension d, and 0 otherwise. To ensure that the parameters have the needed properties, further restrictions of the parameters have to be introduced (cf. Brandt, 2007a, 2008b):

Restriction 1: $\sum_{d=1}^{D} \gamma_{vd} = 0$ for all $v = 1,..., V$ (3)

Restriction 2: $\text{cov}(\theta_v, \gamma_{vd}) = 0$ for all $d = 1,..., D$ (4)

Restriction 3: $\sum_{v=1}^{V} \theta_{vd} = 0$ (5)

Restriction 1 is equivalent to $\dfrac{\sum_{d=1}^{D} \theta_{vd}}{D} = \theta_v$; that is, it assures that θ is the average of persons' absolute abilities in the subdimensions (θ_{vd}). This restriction is essential for correctly identifying the model. Restriction 2, however, is not necessary in this respect; rather, it specifies the composition of the estimate for the main dimension. By constraining all subdimension-specific factors to have the same covariance with the main dimension (namely zero), the subdimensions are defined to be equally weighted for the composition of the main dimension. This practice accords with the common assumption inherent within the bi-factor models described above. It also accords with Humphreys' (1962, 1970, 1981, 1986) recommendation to control differential item functioning or DIF (which arises in the considered case here via the subtests measuring different specific abilities) by balancing across items. Humphreys is supported in this opinion by Wainer, Sireci, and Thissen (1991), who also address the difficulty of this task. Finally, Restriction 3 is one of the common restrictions that ensure correct identification of the model. The shown restriction in this case represents the constraint of the mean of the person parameters of the main dimension to zero. However, as an alternative to this restriction, we can constrain the item parameters to have a mean of zero, or we can anchor one or more of the item parameters.

By using Equation (2), we can also formulate the log-odds form of the subdimension model. This results in

$$\log(p_{v1}/p_{vi0}) = \theta_v + \gamma_{vd(i)} - b_i ,$$ (6)

where p_{vi0} denotes the probability of person v giving an incorrect answer to item i, and requires application of Restrictions 1 to 3, described above. Furthermore, the equations stated above for dichotomous items can be extended to

$$\log(p_{vij}/p_{vi(j-1)}) = \theta_v + \gamma_{vd(i)} - b_{ij} ,$$ (7)

for polytomous items, where p_{vij} and $p_{vi(j-1)}$ are the probabilities of scoring j and j-1 (where $j = 1,..., K_i$-1 and K_i is the number of categories for item (i) to item i for person v, respectively, and b_{ij} is the jth step difficulty of item i. By introducing a parameter b_i, called overall item difficulty, and a parameter τ_{ij}, called jth threshold of item i, where

$$b\sigma_{ij} = b_i + (b_{ij} - b_i) = b_i + \tau_{ij} ,$$ (8)

we can express Equation (7) as

$$\log(p_{vij}/p_{vi(j-1)}) = \theta_v + \gamma_{vd(i)} - (b_i + \tau_{ij}) ,$$ (9)

which reduces to the partial credit model (Masters, 1982) when $\gamma_{vd(i)} = 0$. Extending other Rasch models to include a subdimension component, such as the rating scale model (Andrich, 1978) or the linear logistic test model (Fischer, 1973), is straightforward.

By defining weights

$$q_{id} = \frac{u_{id}}{\sum_{d=1}^{D} u_{id+}} ,$$ (10)

where u_{id} is an indicator variable that is 1 if item i is within dimension d and is zero otherwise, and by inserting Equation (1), we can further express Equation (2) as

$$p_{vi} = \frac{\exp\left((\sum_{d=1}^{D} q_{id}\ \theta_{vd}) - b_i\right)}{1 + \exp\left((\sum_{d=1}^{D} q_{id}\ \theta_{vd}) - b_i\right)}$$ (11)

thereby matching the multidimensional Rasch model (Carstensen, 2000; Rost, 1996). We can, in fact, see the subdimension model as a reparameterized multidimensional model, somewhat similar to Masters' partial credit model, which reparameterizes the Rasch model for polytomous items. Note, however, that in the case of the subdimension model, it is not the item parameters but the person parameters that are reparameterized.

Discussion of the Model

To provide more insight into the subdimension model, I now discuss Restriction 1 and Restriction 2 of the model in more detail.

As I mentioned above, the subdimension model allows for correlations between specific abilities, in contrast to (for example) the Rasch testlet model. Instead, the model incorporates a restriction on the sum of the estimates for the specific abilities (Restriction 1)—a characteristic that can constrain the size of the measured variances for the subdimensions, particularly if the differences in the measured variances are very large. For tests with subdimensions of equal variance, however, it has been shown that the subdimension model provides results equivalent to those of the unrestricted multidimensional model (Brandt, 2007a, 2008b), so allowing the subdimension model to be derived through variable transformation.

This attribute is particularly noteworthy in relation to large-scale assessments such as PISA and TIMSS that utilize detailed background information on the students to impute values for the proficiency variable even though a large portion of item responses are missing due to the matrix-sampling of items administered to each student. Within the calibration process of the person parameter estimates, analysts can use this background information as regression parameters on the estimated latent traits, a process that leaves the residual variances of the latent traits reflecting only those parts of the variances that are not attributable to the regression parameters. This situation, in turn, leads to a decrease in the size of the residual (conditional) variance[1] for the latent traits. It also typically results in variances that are closer to one another in size. Use of the subdimension model can therefore be particularly beneficial in these cases.

An important difference between the subdimension model and other bi-factor models such as the Rasch testlet model is evident in the assumptions each holds about the covariances between specific abilities. To make the resulting differences more obvious, let us consider an example of a science assessment consisting of four testlets, each with five items that refer to a common stimulus, and let us additionally assume that the single measurement of each testlet results in the same variance for the distribution of the measured latent trait. (In other words, the subdimension model will yield results equivalent to the unrestricted multidimensional model.) Let us further assume that the stimuli relate to the following different application areas of science—agriculture, medicine, electronics, and environmental pollution. And then let us suppose, for the purposes of this test, that application of the Rasch testlet model leads to variances of var_{T1} to var_{T4} for the testlet-specific dimension and that application of the subdimension model leads to variances of var_{S1} to var_{S4}.

While, for a given test, we may not find it easy to recognize how these two differently measured variances for the same testlet differ, the difference becomes transparent

---

[1] The actual variances for the latent trait, including the explained variances due to the regression parameters, are calculated *post hoc*.

when we assume that a fifth testlet has been added to the test and that this testlet has a higher correlation with one of the already existing testlets than with the remaining three, perhaps because the stimulus relates to the same application area of (say) agriculture as Testlet 1 does. As a consequence, that part of the testlet-specific variance var_{T1} attributable to the application area is equivalent to that of the new Testlet 5. However, because the Rasch testlet model assumes these variances are independent, applying the Rasch testlet model to the test that has all five testlets will not model the specific variance attributable to the application area of agriculture because of the need to comply with the independence assumption concerning the testlet-specific effects. In short, the model will not account for LID because of the application area in question. Hence, in the Rasch testlet model, var_{T1} will be smaller in the test with all five testlets than in the test with just four testlets. An analysis of item-bundle effects for the mathematics achievement test of PISA 2003 showed that the size of the testlet-specific variances for the item bundles included in all tests differed to a considerable extent according to whether certain item bundles were included or excluded from the analysis (Brandt, 2006).

In the subdimension model, however, the variance of var_{S1} will be the same in the test with four and five testlets (subdimensions) if the testlets yield variances of equal size. When the testlets do not show equal variances, the model usually becomes less capable of modeling the local dependencies among the items of the same testlet.[2] The measured specific effects are comparatively stable, however, and do not depend on the content of the other subdimensions (testlets) in the test. Rather, they depend solely on the size of the variances of these subdimensions, a situation that essentially is due to a normalization problem. Because the subdimension model does not assume the independence of the subdimension-specific factors, the model is less sparse than the testlet model.

In the Rasch testlet model, only one parameter (the variance of the testlet-specific effects)[3] has to be estimated, but in the subdimension model, the covariances for all other existing subdimensions have to be estimated as well. Therefore, it is possible to calibrate the Rasch testlet model for even large numbers of testlets. The number of parameters to be estimated for the subdimension model, however, increases in the same way as occurs with those within the unrestricted multidimensional model. In fact, for both models, the same numbers of parameters always have to be estimated given that the subdimension model is essentially a variable transform of the unrestricted multidimensional model. Comparison of the unrestricted multidimensional model and the subdimension model shows that the number of estimated dimensions is equivalent in both models (see the definition of the scoring matrix above). So, if we assume that the ability estimates in both models are constrained to a mean of

---

[2] In certain cases, the subdimension model might be able to yield results equivalent to those of the unrestricted multidimensional model when the variances of the testlets/subdimensions differ (cf. Brandt, 2007a, 2008b).

[3] Because ConQuest uses a marginal maximum likelihood approach for the parameter estimation, and assuming a standard normal distribution for the measured latent traits, only the mean and the variance to the distribution are estimated.

zero for a test with n dimensions, we will not need to estimate the parameters for n-1 covariances in the subdimension model due to Restriction 2. However, unlike the situation with the unrestricted model, we would have to estimate the n-1 additional parameters for the means of the subdimension-specific latent traits. This is because, in the subdimension model, only the ability estimates of the main dimension are constrained to a mean of zero. Thus, the number of parameters to be estimated is always the same for both models.

ESTIMATION USING CONQUEST

Because the MRCMLM includes the subdimension model as a special case (Brandt, 2007a, 2008b), the software ConQuest (Wu et al., 1998) can be used to estimate the model. Although the mathematical definition of the subdimension model given via the MRCMLM is provided in the proof that the subdimension model is a special case of the MRCMLM, it is still necessary to understand the notations used for the definitions of the scoring and design matrices and, furthermore, to be able to define the resulting constraints using ConQuest syntax. Given the complexity of the MRCMLM notation, as well as the need for knowledge about ConQuest, models like those described above, and also the Rasch testlet model (Wang & Wilson, 2005b), are barely accessible to people interested only in applying adequate models to their data and who are less interested in understanding the theoretical definitions and concepts of particular models. Therefore, a main goal of this paper is to fill in this gap relative to the subdimension model and to give a detailed description for calibrating it. To do this, I begin by briefly describing the different given ways of defining or constraining a model via ConQuest.

Basically, ConQuest offers five different ways of defining or constraining a specific model within the MRCMLM:

1. Through the definition of the design matrix, which describes the linear relationship among the items;
2. Through the definition of a scoring matrix, which assigns the items to specific ability dimensions and assigns scores to their response categories;
3. Through the anchoring of the item-difficulty parameters, which can be used not only for linking to other tests but also for identification purposes;
4. Through specification of mean abilities for the population distribution[4] (within ConQuest denoted as regression parameters); and
5. Through anchoring of the variance–covariance matrix.

Although the definition of the scoring matrix is embedded in ConQuest's command language, the remaining four types of specifications are done via imported text files.

---

[4] Because ConQuest uses a marginal maximum likelihood estimation method, the ability distributions for a given population are assumed to be normal.

For standard unidimensional or multidimensional calibrations, ConQuest's command language provides the means by which the analyst can automatically generate the appropriate design matrices and anchorages. It is through the command **model** that the simple Rasch model (**model item;**), the rating scale model (**model item + step;**), the partial credit model (**model item + item*step;**), and other multifaceted models can be defined, and it is through the set constraint command that identification of the model can be set to **items** (i.e., the mean of the item difficulties is set at zero) or **cases** (i.e., the mean of the ability distribution is set at zero).

On completion of other necessary commands concerning the data file to be calibrated and the output files that are to be generated, a ConQuest command file for the calibration of a unidimensional partial credit model looks like this:

```
datafile estimation.dat;        /* Definition of the data file with
                                the students' answers */

format responses 1-40;          /* Columns in the data file that
                                represent the students' answers
                                */

codes 0,1,2;                    /* Definition of valid answer
                                codes-all other codes will be
                                interpreted as missing by design
                                */

score (0,1,2) (0,1,2)!items     /* Definition of the scoring
(1-40);                         matrix (here, according to a
                                unidimensional model)*/

model item + item*step;         /* Definition of the design matrix
                                (here, according to the partial
                                credit model) */

set constraints = items;        /* Constraint for the identification
                                of the model */

export designmatrix >>          /* Export of the design matrix
estimation.dsm;                 to a data file with the given name
                                */

estimate;                       /* Start of the calibration using
                                the standard settings /*

show >> estimation.shw;         /* Export of the calibration
                                results to a data file with the
                                given name   */
```

This example assumes that the answer data provided by the data file has already been scored and that a single digit represents each coded answer. Thus, each column represents the students' answers to a particular item, scored with 0, 1, or 2 credits (cf. also the **code** statement above).[5] In the unidimensional case, the scoring matrix reduces to a simple vector (with 40 elements) that maps all scores on all items to the same dimension.

In regard to the definition of the design matrix via the **model** command, note that if the model is constrained to have a mean item difficulty of zero (as in the above case), the design matrix will have to be changed accordingly. Therefore, the design matrix will not be generated until the start of the calibration in order to comply with the given **set constraint** command. As for the unidimensional calibration conducted by the above command file, the **export designmatrix** command is not necessary. Nevertheless, this statement is valuable here because the design matrix generated for the calibration is exactly the design matrix needed in order to define the subdimension model presented below.[6] Finally, the **estimate** command starts the calibration with the standard algorithm and convergence criteria of ConQuest, and the show command generates a standard output for the results of the calibration, written to a text file named "estimation.shw".

Defining models like the subdimension model requires somewhat more effort since there is no ConQuest command to automatically generate and set the necessary constraints according to the model definitions. Instead, this has to be done manually by providing appropriate import files. The main focus of this section, therefore, is to describe the construction and definition of these import files as well as the definition of the specific scoring matrix needed for the model.

```
datafile estimation.dat;      /* See above */
format responses 1-40;        /* See above */
codes 0,1,2;                  /* See above */

score (0,1,2) (0,1,2) (0,1,2) () () !items (1-10);
score (0,1,2) (0,1,2) () (0,1,2) () !items (11-20);
score (0,1,2) (0,1,2) () () (0,1,2) !items (21-30);
score (0,1,2) (0,1,2) (0,-1,-2)(0,-1,-2) (0,-1,-2)!items (31-40);
                              /* Definition of the scoring matrix */

model item + item*step;       /* Pseudo-definition of the design
                                 matrix */

import designmatrix <<        /* Actual definition of the design
estimation.dsm;                  matrix */

import anchor_covariance      /* Setting of the constraints for
<< estimation.cov;               the variance-covariance matrix */

estimate !method=             /* Start of the calibration using a
montecarlo,nodes=2000;          Monte Carlo method with 2000 nodes
                                 and standard convergence criteria */
```

---

[5] ConQuest also provides a way of scoring the data via the command language; more information about these commands can be found in the ConQuest manual.

[6] If the design matrix has not been generated at the time the command is processed, ConQuest exports the file as soon as the design matrix is generated; that is, after the start of the calibration.

```
show >> estimation.shw;    /* Export of the calibration results
                              to a data file with the given name
                              */
```

The first three commands of the command file correspond to those of the unidimensional calibration above; that is, the same data-set as the one above is calibrated. Here, it is assumed that the test includes four subtests with 10 items each, with Items 1 to 10 referring to Subtest 1, Items 11 to 20 to Subtest 2, Items 21 to 30 to Subtest 3, and Items 31 to 40 to Subtest 4. In order to account for the assumed local dependencies between the items of the same subtest, the subdimension model is used for estimation. As the definition of the scoring matrix above shows, the subdimension model is a multidimensional model; in the above example, it has four dimensions. The first dimension, comparable to the unidimensional case above, refers to the unidimensional latent trait that all 40 items commonly measure. The second and fourth dimensions, however, refer to the specific parameters of the subdimensions that are to be estimated. According to Restriction 1 of the definition of the subdimension model, the subdimension-specific parameters must add up to zero for each student. In order to comply with this restriction, the parameter estimates of the fourth subdimension cannot directly be estimated but rather defined as constrained parameters. When the sum of the four subdimension-specific parameters is zero, then each person's fourth parameter (or any single other of the four) always equals the negative of the sum of the other three parameters. What this means, in essence, is that the subdimension model actually contains only $d-1$-estimated *specific* dimensions, and one final specific dimension, which is totally determined by the negative sum of the previous $d-1$. Therefore, Items 1 to 10 load (in addition to the main dimension) on Dimension 2, Items 11 to 20 load on Dimension 3, Items 31 to 40 load on Dimension 3, and Items 31 to 40 load negatively on Dimensions 2 to 4.

The model statement follows the process involved in defining the scoring matrix. This statement has only a dummy function, which exists for programming reasons, given that ConQuest's **estimate** command must always be preceded by a **model** command. The design matrix generated according to this standard statement cannot be used because it is problematic in two ways. First, for items that load on more than one dimension, ConQuest adjusts the design matrix in order to keep the difficulty estimates of the items in proportion to the size of the ability estimates. In the case of the subdimension model, this step simply results in estimates that are exactly half the size of the unidimensional estimates, thereby making comparisons just that little bit more difficult. Secondly, ConQuest does not adjust the design matrix according to the necessary constraint of the item parameters needed for the subdimension model. The needed constraint is correctly defined, though, in the design matrix generated for the corresponding unidimensional calibration. Furthermore, by using this design matrix, the software renders the parameter estimates of the calibration for the subdimension model comparable to those of the unidimensional model, and it does this without any further linear transformation. Therefore, the easiest and (probably) least error-inducing way to obtain the correct design matrix is to generate it with the corresponding unidimensional model, as shown in the example above.

Once the correct design matrix is imported, all that remains to do is correctly anchor the variance–covariance matrix according to Restriction 2 of the model. This step requires creation and importation of an appropriate text file. For the above example, the import file "estimation.cov" has the following format:

```
1        2      0.0000
1        3      0.0000
1        4      0.0000
```

The first two figures in a row define which covariance is to be set. Thus, in the first row above (the covariance of Dimensions 1 and 2), the third figure sets the value for the given covariance. Here, all listed covariances are set at zero, a practice that aligns with the definition of the subdimension model, which requires the covariances between the main dimension and the subdimensions to be constrained to zero.

The empirical example presented in the next section was calibrated using ConQuest, as described in this section.

AN EMPIRICAL EXAMPLE

The empirical example given here is based on data taken from the mathematics achievement test used for TIMSS 2003 (Mullis, Martin, Gonzales, & Chrostowski, 2004; Mullis et al., 2003). This test was developed according to two different aspects—a content domain and a cognitive domain. While the latter domain consisted of *knowing facts and procedures, using concepts, solving routine problems,* and *reasoning*, the analysis presented in the following refers to the five defined content domains, which were *number, algebra, measurement, geometry*, and *data*. To select appropriate items for the main study, the TIMSS researchers conducted a full-scale field trial. They then used the results of this trial to determine which items would be used in the main study. During this selection process, the researchers took care not only to distribute the items across the four cognitive and five content domains according to the proportions defined in the assessment framework but also to ensure that the psychometric characteristics of the items were sufficient, particularly in relation to DIF effects and discrimination power (Martin et al., 2004).

Because the psychometric criteria chosen refer to a unidimensional analysis of the data, we can consider the test to have been constructed as multidimensional from a qualitative point of view, via the *ex ante* defined domains, and as unidimensional from a quantitative measurement point of view. The described test construction displays the dilemma of TIMSS and other large-scale assessments associated with lack of appropriate models (cf. the test construction for the PISA study, for example; OECD, 2005). The resulting data-sets, therefore, are not good examples of true multidimensionality. Despite this, the assessment results are publicly reported and interpreted. With these considerations in mind, the following analysis shows the extent to which the subdimension model can still help provide more appropriate measures by modeling the five content domains defined for the mathematics test.

Data and Analysis

The analyzed test used data obtained from the United States sub-sample of students who participated in TIMSS 2003. This sub-sample consisted of 8,912 students in total, and the test included 194 mathematics items: 47 items for the content domain *algebra*, 28 for *data*, 32 items for *geometry*, 31 for *measurement*, and 56 for *number*. Nineteen of the 194 items were partial-credit items, each with three score categories. In order to compare and discuss the results obtained via the subdimension model (more precisely its extension to the partial credit model), I also analyzed the data using the unidimensional model, the testlet model, and the (unrestricted) multidimensional model.

Results and Discussion

Table 1 summarizes the results of the estimated means[7] and variances for the distributions, their reliabilities, the correlations, and the -2 log likelihoods for the different models. The index M (main dimension) refers to the unidimensional latent trait; the indices 1 to 5 refer to the content domains algebra, data, geometry, measurement, and number, respectively.

On comparing the variance obtained for the main dimension of the subdimension model with the variance obtained via the unidimensional model, we find that the actual variance is underestimated in the unidimensional case because of the local dependencies of the items of the same content domain. Although the test was constructed to be unidimensional, the subdimension model shows an increase in measured variance. The variance rises from 1.19 to 1.25, which is equivalent to an increase of about 5%. The increase in variance accords with findings by other authors (e.g., Sireci et al., 1991; Wang & Wilson, 2005b; Yen, 1993). If we look at the given reliabilities for the main dimensions, it becomes even clearer that the reliability given for the ability estimates is overestimated in the unidimensional case. Despite the subdimension model allowing for a gain in measured variance, the given reliability of its estimates is still lower than that of the unidimensional estimates. Essentially, the true reliability of the ability estimates calculated via the unidimensional model is *smaller* than that given for the main dimension of the subdimension model.

A difference between the multidimensional model and the subdimension model that becomes apparent on looking at the results is that the absolute variances of the latent traits measured by the subtests are closer to one another when the subdimension model is used than when the multidimensional model is used. While use of the multidimensional model shows subtest variances ranging from 0.86 to 1.74, the (absolute) variances obtained using the subdimension model range from only 1.35 to 1.40. This difference reflects the inability of the subdimension model to fully model the differences between the subtests due to their different variances. The estimated likelihoods of the two models provide a further indication of the extent to which the

---

[7] The means and correlations for the testlet model given in Table 1 are not estimated but instead display the anchor values of the parameters; the testlet model is constrained on the cases, given that this constraint is the only one that yields an optimum model fit.

Table 1: Results of the reanalysis of the US TIMSS 2003 mathematics achievement test

	Unidim.		Testlet		Subdim.		Multidim.	
Parameter	Estimate	Reliability	Estimate	Reliability	Estimate	Reliability	Estimate	Reliability
σ^2_M	1.19	0.820	1.22	0.812	1.25	0.816		
$\sigma^2_1 / \sigma^2_{S1}$			0.21	0.141	0.14	0.148	1.45	0.767
$\sigma^2_2 / \sigma^2_{S2}$			0.19	0.103	0.13	0.113	1.74	0.757
$\sigma^2_3 / \sigma^2_{S3}$			0.15	0.096	0.15	0.145	0.86	0.722
$\sigma^2_4 / \sigma^2_{S4}$			0.08	0.053	0.10	0.107	1.48	0.781
$\sigma^2_5 / \sigma^2_{S5}$*			0.07	0.062	0.05		1.41	0.800
μ_M	0.02		0.00		0.00			
μ_1 / μ_{S1}			0.00		0.12		-0.04	
μ_2 / μ_{S2}			0.00		0.29		0.43	
μ_3 / μ_{S3}			0.00		-0.29		-0.15	
μ_4 / μ_{S4}			0.00		-0.20		-0.29	
μ_5 / μ_{S5}*			0.00		0.09		0.12	
r_{12} / r_{S12}			0.00		-0.32		0.88	
r_{13} / r_{S13}			0.00		-0.26		0.85	
r_{14} / r_{S14}			0.00		-0.49		0.87	
r_{15} / r_{S15}*			0.00		-0.03		0.92	
r_{23} / r_{S23}			0.00		-0.36		0.84	
r_{24} / r_{S24}			0.00		-0.26		0.90	
r_{25} / r_{S25}*			0.00		-0.14		0.90	
r_{34} / r_{S34}			0.00		-0.14		0.90	
r_{35} / r_{S35}*			0.00		-0.51		0.89	
r_{45} / r_{S45}*			0.00		0.09		0.95	
Estimated Param.	214		219		228		228	
-2 Log Likelihood	275738.4		275380.2		275311.4		275022.6	

Note: * Calculated via plausible values.

subdimension model is capable of modeling the differences between the subtests. The likelihood deviances (-2 log likelihood) of using the multidimensional and the subdimension models are 275,022.6 and 275,311.4, respectively. The likelihood deviance for the unidimensional model, however, is 275,738.4; its difference of just 715.8 within the multidimensional model reflects the unidimensional construction of the measure. Nevertheless, the subdimension model does close the gap between the unidimensional and the multidimensional by about 50%.

Besides the differences in measurement precision and model fit, the interpretational differences of the measures provided by the two models should be of particular interest to test developers and analysts. In the case of the subdimension model, it is not the reliabilities of the *total* subtests that are measured but the reliabilities of the differences *between* the subtests. This is particularly interesting if the tests are being used to analyze, for example, student profiles constructed via the subtests.

Here, the reliabilities provide a measure of how reliable differentiating these students according to these profiles will be and so help develop tests that provide especially reliable measures in these terms.

For the given empirical example, the results with subtest-specific reliabilities ranging from 0.107 to 0.148 indicate that an interpretation of the subtest-specific variances—that is, of differences between the subtests—need to be interpreted with caution. On the other hand, the correlation estimates for the subtest-specific variances provided by the subdimension model bring greater transparency to the differences between the subtests. In the multidimensional model, the large proportion of common variance dominates the correlation estimates, and these differ, at most, by 0.11 (from 0.84 to 0.95), and the estimated correlations for the subdimension model differ by up to 0.60 (from -0.51 to 0.09). Nevertheless, the interpretation of the usually negative correlations provided by the subdimension model (resulting from the applied constraint) is not as intuitive. This is because a correlation of close to 0 for the relative subdimension-specific parameters is usually equivalent to a very high correlation of the corresponding absolute ability estimates. An example of this relationship is provided via Dimensions 4 and 5 above. Although their estimated correlation in the multidimensional model is given as 0.95, the corresponding correlation in the subdimension model is 0.09. This example is a very unusual case of positive correlation. Moreover, when compared with the other subtest correlations within the test, it represents a particularly high correlation between the two dimensions.

As a further comparison, and in order to show other differences, I also applied the testlet model to the data. The comparison of the likelihood deviances showed that, even given the very unfavorable conditions for the subdimension model due to the large difference between the smallest and the largest estimated variances, the model under discussion outperformed the testlet model. The difficulties for the testlet model to appropriately model the given data are best displayed by the relationship between Dimensions 4 and 5. As the results of the multidimensional analysis show, the correlation between these two dimensions is, on average, over 0.05 higher than the correlations between the remaining dimensions. While the subdimension model allows for any specific variance the dimensions have in common, the testlet model constrains the covariance of the respective testlet dimensions to zero. In other words, the large common part of their specific variances is not modeled and, in turn, the modeled variance is comparatively small; in the above example, it is less than half that modeled for the other dimensions.

In summary, the results of the reanalysis show that the application of the subdimension model allows for an increase in measurement precision for the students' unidimensional parameter estimates despite the very unfavorable conditions. Furthermore, the above results indicate that, for the analyses conducted above, the parameter estimates from the multidimensional model yield higher measurement precision for researchers endeavoring to interpret a person's abilities relative to the subtests.

CONCLUSION

The subdimension model offers test developers and analysts a way of handling the common conflict between theory and practice that arises whenever both unidimensional and multidimensional ability estimates of the same test are needed. Hitherto, tests were usually constructed in a unidimensional manner even if they included subtests that supposedly incorporated different characteristics. This practice meant that expected differences between these subtests due to test construction were minimized. Thus, any items particularly adept at showing differences between the subtests would probably not comply with the (unidimensional) psychometric criteria used within the selection process after field trial of the items. Therefore, in order to gain interpretational value for the analysis of the subtests, psychometric criteria need to be based on a model that explicitly accounts for the differences in the subtests. The subdimension model provides exactly this opportunity. By allowing for correlations between the subtest-specific factors, the model is particularly effective in accounting for differences and is able to outperform more restrictive models, like the testlet model (see discussions above).

Due to the restriction of the subdimension-specific parameters to yield a mean of zero, the correlations obtained under the subdimension model cannot be compared directly with those of the multidimensional model. For tests with large differences in subtest variances, this restriction also hinders the ability of the subdimension model to model, to full extent, the LID brought about by the different subtests. The advantages of the model become particularly apparent, however, when the variances of the measured subdimensions are approximately equal. In these cases, the subdimension model yields results almost equivalent to those of the unrestricted multidimensional model. With large-scale assessment studies that use matrix-sampling for administering the items and detailed background information for estimating person parameters, the chances of obtaining favorable conditions for the subdimension model are particularly high. Additionally, and/or in other cases, it might also be possible to provide more favorable conditions by adjusting the subtests for the differences in variances apparent after the field trial and by, for example, using different numbers of items for each subtest.

Another benefit of the subdimension model becomes apparent in regard to large-scale assessments when the matrix sampling for items is used. In these cases, each student receives only one booklet containing a subset of items, which means that several different booklets are needed to administer all items. (TIMSS 2003 used 12 different booklets.) The construction of these booklets typically endeavors to link the items that measure the same construct and to balance item-difficulty differences due to positional effects. An additional balancing of the booklets according to the number of items from the same subtest is usually not feasible. In this instance, the various booklets frequently end up including more items of a particular subtest and fewer of another. A student who performs particularly well in one subtest and poorly in another will effectively get different scores for the overall test depending on the booklet he or she completed. More specifically, this is because the common unidimensional Rasch model does not account for differences in sets of items due to different subtests.

The subdimension model, however, accounts for these differences, and thereby yields more adequate individual measures. Although researchers conducting large-scale assessments are usually not interested in achievement scores for single students, estimation of adequate ability estimates for single students is important because the calculation of adequate correlations (e.g., between a person's achievement score and his or her socioeconomic background) depends on adequate scores at the single-person level.

In addition to its ability to analyze tests measuring a general domain and multiple sub-domains at the same time, the subdimension model seems to provide benefits for other applications. The application for vertical scaling, for example, is straightforward, with the subtests representing tests given at different points in time. However, future research in this area needs to investigate how results arising from use of the subdimension model relate to other models used for vertical scaling. Furthermore, and beyond its application to empirical data, the subdimension model could be usefully employed in simulation studies because of its ability to provide additional and more subtle information, as some of my recent work shows (Brandt, 2007b, 2008a).

Finally, another way of using the subdimension model could be to adjust Restriction 2 of the model so that the measured subtests are not balanced within the overall measure but instead are "assigned" (per definition) more weight—or relevance—than others, which means the characteristics of such models would have to be investigated as well. By providing a detailed description on how to calibrate the subdimension model using ConQuest, I hope that the gap between the development of new models and their application in practice becomes somewhat smaller and that a larger community than at present finds conducting research and practice via a model like the subdimension model a considerably more accessible proposition.

References

Adams, R. J., Wilson, M., & Wang, W. C. (1997). The multidimensional random coefficients multinomial logit model. *Applied Psychological Measurement, 21*(1), 1–23.

Andrich, D. (1978). A rating formulation for ordered response categories. *Psychometrika, 43*(4), 561–573.

Brandt, S. (2006). *Exploring bundle dependencies for the embedded attitudinal items in PISA 2006.* Paper presented at the International Objective Measurement Workshop (IOMW), Berkeley, CA.

Brandt, S. (2007a). *Applications of a Rasch model with subdimensions.* Paper presented at the 2007 annual conference of the American Educational Research Association (AERA), Chicago, IL.

Brandt, S. (2007b). *Item bundles with items relating to different subtests and their influence on subtests' measurement characteristics.* Paper presented at the 2007 annual conference of the American Educational Research Association (AERA), Chicago, IL.

Brandt, S. (2008a). *The impact of local-item dependence on multidimensional analyses.* Paper submitted for publication.

Brandt, S. (2008b). *Modeling tests with subtests*. Paper submitted for publication.

Carstensen, C. H. (2000). *Mehrdimensionale Testmodelle mit Anwendungen aus der pädagogisch-psychologischen Diagnostik (Multidimensional test models with applications from educational and psychological diagnostics)*. Kiel: Leibniz Institute for Science Education (IPN).

Fischer, G. H. (1973). The linear logistic test model as an instrument in educational research. *Acta Psychologica, 37*, 359–374.

Gibbons, R. D., Bock, R. D., Hedeker, D., Weiss, D. J., Segawa, E., Bhaumik, D. K., et al. (2007). Full-information item bi-factor analysis of graded response data. *Applied Psychological Measurement, 31*(4), 4–19.

Gibbons, R. D., & Hedeker, D. (1992). Full-information item bi-factor analysis. *Psychometrika, 57*, 423–436.

Holzinger, K. J., & Swineford, F. (1937). The bi-factor method. *Psychometrika, 2*, 41–54.

Humphreys, L. G. (1962). The organization of human abilities. *American Psychologist, 17*, 475–483.

Humphreys, L. G. (1970). A skeptical look at the factor pure test. In C. E. Lunneborg (Ed.), *Current problems and techniques in multivariate psychology: Proceedings of a conference honoring Professor Paul Horst* (pp. 22–32). Seattle, WA: University of Washington.

Humphreys, L. G. (1981). The primary mental ability. In M. P. Friedman, J. P. Das, & N. O'Connor (Eds.), *Intelligence and learning* (pp. 87–102). New York: Plenum.

Humphreys, L. G. (1986). An analysis and evaluation of test and item bias in the prediction context. *Journal of Applied Social Psychology, 71*, 327–333.

Martin, M. O., Mullis, I. V. S., & Chrostowski, S. J. (Eds.). (2004). *TIMSS 2003 technical report*. Chestnut Hill, MA: Boston College.

Masters, G. N. (1982). A Rasch model for partial credit scoring. *Psychometrika, 47*(2), 149–174.

Mullis, I. V., Martin, M. O., Gonzales, E. J., & Chrostowski, S. J. (Eds.). (2004). *TIMSS 2003 international mathematics report*. Chestnut Hill, MA: Boston College.

Mullis, I. V., Martin, M. O., Smith, T. A., Garden, R. A., Gregory, K. D., Gonzales, E. J., et al. (2003). *TIMSS assessment frameworks and specifications 2003* (2nd ed.). Chestnut Hill, MA: Boston College.

Muraki, E., & Carlson, J. E. (1995). Full-information factor analysis for polytomous item responses. *Applied Psychological Measurement, 19*, 73–90.

Organisation for Economic Co-operation and Development (OECD). (2005). *PISA 2003 technical report*. Paris: Author.

Rasch, G. (1980). *Probabilistic models for some intelligence and attainment tests*. Chicago: University of Chicago Press.

Rost, J. (1996). *Lehrbuch Testtheorie, Testkonstruktion (Textbook test theory, test construction)*. Bern, Göttingen, Toronto, Seattle, WA: Verlag Hans Huber.

Sireci, S. G., Thissen, D., & Wainer, H. (1991). On the reliability of testlet-based tests. *Journal of Educational Measurement, 28*(3), 237–247.

Thissen, D., Steinberg, L., & Mooney, J. A. (1989). Trace lines for testlets: A use of multiple-categorical-response models. *Journal of Educational Measurement, 26*(3), 247–260.

Wainer, H., & Kiely, G. (1987). Item clusters and computerized adaptive testing: A case for testlets. *Journal of Educational Measurement, 24*, 185–202.

Wainer, H., Sireci, S. G., & Thissen, D. (1991). Differential testlet functioning: Definitions and detection. *Journal of Educational Measurement, 28*(3), 197–219.

Wang, W.-C., & Wilson, M. (2005a). Exploring local item dependence using a random-effects facet model. *Applied Psychological Measurement, 29*(4), 296–318.

Wang, W.-C., & Wilson, M. (2005b). The Rasch testlet model. *Applied Psychological Measurement, 29*(2), 126–149.

Wu, M. L., Adams, R. J., & Wilson, M. R. (1998). *ACER ConQuest: Generalized item response modeling software.* Melbourne, VIC: Australian Council for Educational Research.

Yen, W. M. (1993). Scaling performance assessments: Strategies for managing local item dependence. *Journal of Educational Measurement, 30*(3), 187–213.

Application of multilevel IRT to investigate cross-national skill profiles on TIMSS 2003

Chanho Park and Daniel M. Bolt
University of Wisconsin-Madison, USA

This article presents a multilevel IRT model developed for group-level diagnosis and applied to study cross-national profiles on the TIMSS 2003 mathematics assessment. Variability in item difficulty (i.e., differential item functioning or DIF) across countries is investigated in relation to item features associated with content and cognitive process categories. Random effects were attached to each feature type at the country level, and their variability studied across countries. The estimated feature effects were shown to provide a basis for examining cross-national differences for individual features as well as cross-feature differences within individual countries, as may be useful for diagnostic purposes. The model was fitted using a Markov chain Monte Carlo (MCMC) procedure implemented in WinBUGS.

INTRODUCTION

Educational tests are frequently designed to enable comparisons between units at different levels of an educational hierarchy. For example, while many tests are designed to compare individual student performances, others are designed to facilitate comparisons at a higher level (e.g., among schools, districts, states, or countries). Assessments such as the Trends in International Mathematics and Science Study (TIMSS), the Programme for International Student Assessment (PISA), and the National Assessment of Educational Progress (NAEP), for instance, are designed to facilitate comparisons among units above the student level. The best use of the assessments is achieved when statistical methodologies designed for inferences at the appropriate level(s) of comparison are used. The purpose of this study was to propose and investigate a statistical modeling approach based on application of multilevel item response theory (ML-IRT) for group-level diagnosis.

Our real data application of the model used item response data from TIMSS. The aim of the TIMSS assessments is "to improve the teaching and learning of mathematics and science by providing data about students' achievement in relation to different types of curricula, instructional practices, and school environments" (Mullis, Martin, Gonzalez, & Chrostowski, 2004, p. 13). Both the mathematics and science tests are designed to provide comparative information regarding cross-national achievement, in the hope that educators and policy-makers use the information to evaluate the effectiveness of their respective curricula and to provide better education to their students. Cross-national comparisons based on TIMSS can be made not only in overall mathematics and science abilities, but also in specific areas related to particular content and cognitive domains. Indeed, it is through these more specific diagnoses that more meaningful information able to underpin improvements to educational practice might be attained. For example, the mathematics assessment in TIMSS organizes items according to five content domains—number, algebra, measurement, geometry, and data—and four cognitive domains—knowing facts and procedures, using concepts, solving routine problems, and reasoning. Each item is assigned to one content domain category and one cognitive domain category. Currently, TIMSS reports domain scale scores with respect to these content and cognitive domains as well as overall scores (Mullis et al., 2004; Mullis, Martin, & Foy, 2005). It is important to note, however, that because all items are cross-classified into both content and cognitive categories, there is the potential for some confounding of effects when attempting to interpret scores specific to each domain. The goal of this study was to present an item response theory (IRT)-based methodology that would explain differential item functioning (DIF) in relation to the content and cognitive characteristics of the items, and in the process better distinguish these effects by controlling for effects related to one characteristic when examining the effects of another.

IRT has provided a useful scaling methodology for educational measurement, and has also found useful applications to the TIMSS assessment, as well as to similarly designed large-scale assessments (e.g., NAEP, PISA). A common strategy entails the introduction of a separate proficiency for each student with respect to each domain (possibly handled simultaneously within a multidimensional model). Due to the matrix sampling designs used with these assessments, a plausible values methodology (often adding student background variables as covariates) is used to account for the varying amounts of uncertainty of each student's level of attainment on each proficiency. Group-level (e.g., country-level) estimates of proficiency distribution parameters (i.e., mean, standard deviation) can then be derived, often incorporating sampling weights. The current approach to domain score reporting using TIMSS data appears to follow this general approach (Mullis et al., 2005). Various issues related to model estimation with this type of design have been described by von Davier, Sinharay, Oranje, and Beaton (2007) in the context of NAEP.

While this modeling approach is a very natural strategy, others may also prove useful. As noted, one potential challenge with this approach when using TIMSS mathematics items is the tendency for items from different cognitive domains to belong disproportionately to different content domains. The introduction of distinct IRT scaling models for each domain can thus make it difficult to disentangle the relative contribution of content-domain versus cognitive-domain effects when interpreting each scale. Perhaps a more general limitation is the challenge associated with determining the appropriate number and type of proficiencies to introduce into the model. Highly intercorrelated proficiencies may be better handled statistically in the form of a single unidimensional model (see Haberman & von Davier, 2007, for a discussion of these issues). In addition, there is no guarantee that the multiple proficiencies that may best distinguish students from one another within a country are also those that best distinguish groups (e.g., countries) from one another. Indeed, the TIMSS cognitive domain scores tend to show high intercorrelations at the country level (Mullis et al., 2005).

Other IRT-based procedures for group-level diagnostic assessment have been proposed for TIMSS subscore reporting. Tatsuoka, Corter, and Tatsuoka (2004; see also Chen, Gorin, Thompson, & Tatsuoka, this volume pp. 23–49) applied the rule-space methodology for this purpose. They identified 23 skill attributes that were assumed to fully explain the mathematics item difficulties for Grade 8 students in a revised version of TIMSS administered in 1999. Using these attributes, Tatsuoka and her colleagues presented mathematical content and process skill profiles for a sample of participating countries. For example, they found United States students to be weak in geometry, a content area that "does correlate highly with the attributes measuring higher order mathematical thinking" (2004, p. 920). One potential limitation of this approach is that it appears to be based on an aggregation of student-level diagnoses, which can vary considerably in their reliability across skills.

Other approaches may be used to address these limitations and build alternative frameworks for domain score reporting. In this article, we consider a ML-IRT model for DIF as the basis for score reports. Researchers have observed that IRT models can be viewed as a type of hierarchical generalized linear model (Raudenbush & Bryk, 2002) or, alternatively, as a generalized linear or nonlinear mixed model (Rijmen, Tuerlinckx, De Boeck, & Kuppens, 2003; see also McCulloch & Searle, 2001, for a general description of linear and nonlinear mixed models). By viewing item parameters as fixed effects and person ability parameters as random effects, we can portray traditional IRT models as two-level models or mixed models. This modeling framework accommodates higher grouping levels that, in turn, give rise to multilevel IRT models. For example, Kamata (2001, 2002) demonstrated how the one-parameter logistic (1PL) model or the Rasch model can be represented as a two-level generalized linear model and successfully extended it to a three-level model (see also Cheong & Raudenbush, 2000). ML-IRT has thus been used as a hierarchical extension of traditional IRT models (Adams, Wilson, & Wu, 1997) or as applications of the multilevel paradigm to IRT (Fox, 2003; Fox & Glas, 2001). One advantage of this multilevel representation is that it becomes possible to build in additional levels (e.g., classroom, school, etc.) that might be associated with test performance (De Boeck & Wilson, 2004). Such contextual factors may influence not only the distribution of ability within the population, but also characteristics of the test items, such as item difficulty. As described below, ML-IRT also makes it possible to model item difficulty with respect to multiple item characteristics simultaneously, thus enabling us to understand group differences on more features than would be achievable through computing domain scores.

One alternative ML-IRT approach to reporting profile scores could effectively use DIF at a group (e.g., country) level as a basis for skill profile reports. As an example of this type of approach, Prowker and Camilli (2007) developed an item difficulty variation (IDV) model as an application of a generalized linear mixed model. This model is characterized by the allowance of random effects for item parameters. Items with substantial variability in difficulty are detected, and the cause of variation can be interpreted using contextual factors, such as how well an item matches a state's curriculum standards.

The focus of the current study is on interpreting DIF in relation to item features. Like Prowker and Camilli (2007), we assume that an item's tendency to display DIF can provide diagnostic information of relevance for score reporting purposes. Unlike the Prowker and Camilli (2007) IDV model, however, our approach seeks to model DIF in relation to item characteristics that are explicitly added to the model to account for difficulty variation across countries and that are assumed to be of value for score reporting purposes.

A MULTILEVEL ITEM FEATURE MODEL AND EXAMPLE ILLUSTRATION

As noted, the purpose of our study was to develop a new ML-IRT methodology and to illustrate its application in a study of cross-national differences on the TIMSS 2003 Grade 8 mathematics assessment. The current illustration of the methodology is somewhat simplistic, and ignores features of the model that might be added (e.g., an account for sampling weights, school effects) to more accurately reflect the TIMSS assessment and its sampling design. However, the illustration allows us to demonstrate in a general way how average skill profiles associated with different countries could be reported using the methodology. Central to the current application is the coding of items according to characteristics that can help provide an explanation of cross-national differences. We refer to the current model as an item feature model (IFM), and we recognize that there are various other ways of attempting to model country-to-country variability in item difficulty.

The IFM assumes the items can be coded according to what we refer to as *item features*. As noted earlier, the Grade 8 mathematics items on TIMSS are currently categorized according to content and cognitive features. Each item can be classified into exactly one category for each feature. In this model, the TIMSS item content and cognitive categories are studied as potential contributors to DIF across countries. In a multilevel modeling framework, the model is a three-level one in which item responses are nested within students and students are nested within countries. In the current ML-IRT model, ability is assumed to vary both at the student and the country levels; item difficulty is assumed to vary only at the country level, with each item assumed to have the same difficulty parameter across students from the same country. The objective in fitting the IFM is to investigate features that demonstrate variability across countries.

As mentioned, in the TIMSS item feature categorization, items generally belong to more than one category. Consequently, attempts to study cross-national differences by grouping items (e.g., subscale reporting) may not be appropriate, as the different item characteristics are frequently confounded. This situation makes the currently proposed ML-IRT model a potentially more beneficial way of studying cross-national differences.[1] The next section details the statistical model that is the basis for studying item feature effects across countries.

MULTILEVEL STRUCTURE OF THE IFM

A multilevel representation of the IFM results in a decomposition of item response variance across three levels, with repeated measures (items) nested within students, and students nested within countries. The statistical representation of the model is as follows. At Level 1:

$$P\left(X_{ijk} = 1 \mid \theta_{jk}\right) = \frac{\exp\left(\theta_{jk} - b_{ik}\right)}{1 + \exp\left(\theta_{jk} - b_{ik}\right)} \quad ,$$

where $X_{ijk} = 1$ denotes a correct response by student j from country k to item i (partial credit items were recoded so that 0, 1=0 and 2=1),

θ_{jk} is the ability level of student j in country k,

b_{ik} is the difficulty parameter for item i when administered to students in country k.

At Level 2:

$$\theta_{jk} = \mu_k + E_{jk},$$

where μ_k denotes the mean ability level in country k, and

E_{jk} is assumed to be normally distributed with a mean of 0 and a variance of σ_k^2.

Finally, at Level 3:

$$\mu_k = \gamma_0 + U_k,$$

$$b_{ik} = \delta_{i1} + \sum_l w_{kl} q_{il}, \ k = 1, \ ..., \ K,$$

where K is the number of countries,

δ_{i1} is the difficulty of item i for country 1 (a reference country),

q_{il} is an indicator variable, indicating whether (content or cognitive) feature l (= 1, ..., L) is associated with item i, and

w_{kl} are continuous variables identifying the effect of feature l on the difficulty of items within country k; $w_{11}, ..., w_{iL} = 0$.

---

[1] The coding of item features for the 99 released mathematics items for Grade 8 is available from the TIMSS website (http://timss.bc.edu/PDF/T03_RELEASED_M8.pdf).

Note that the item difficulties within each country (except for the reference country) are defined relative to those of the reference country for statistical identification purposes (more detail on identification of the model appears in the next section) and to ensure a comparable interpretation of θ across countries. The model includes fixed effects associated with the overall ability mean across countries (γ_0), and item difficulties for the reference country (δ_{i1}). The w_{kl} are (potentially random) effects associated with each attribute. When normalized, these random effects are assumed to be normal, with a mean of zero and an estimated variance of τ_r^2 The U_k are assumed to be normally distributed, with a mean of zero and a variance of τ_0^2.

MODEL IDENTIFICATION

It is well known that IRT models are over-parameterized and that the estimated model parameters are thus identifiable only up to a linear transformation (Embretson & Reise, 2000; Hambleton & Swaminathan, 1985). Because item parameters are considered structural parameters and ability parameters incidental parameters (Hambleton & Swaminathan, 1985), it is common practice in IRT to fix the metric of the ability parameters (θ) to resolve the indeterminacy. However, the indeterminacy can also be resolved by assuming the item difficulty parameters have a specified mean and variance. In the current application, we addressed the indeterminacy of the θ metric by assigning the difficulty parameters a mean of zero in a reference country (the United States). Next, to make the θ metrics for other countries determinate, we assumed the item parameters for items of a particular type (as defined by a reference content feature and a reference cognitive feature) to be invariant across countries. In the current application, these items were defined by the "data" content category and the "using concepts" cognitive category. Consequently, for each country, there were a total of four free deviations estimated among the content categories and three deviations among cognitive categories. It is important to note that we assumed the "data" and "using concepts" items to be invariant only in order to define an initial metric against which all remaining model parameters could be uniquely estimated. As noted below, we later rescaled the solutions by normalizing the effects of the item features within each country (thus allowing the "data" and "using concepts" items to also have varying difficulties across countries).

The reason for defining linking items according to both a content feature and a cognitive feature can be attributed to the rank deficiency of the item feature incidence matrix (the elements q_{il} at Level 3). As noted above, each of the TIMSS Grade 8 mathematics items is categorized with respect to exactly one content feature and one cognitive feature. Thus, the item feature incidence matrix of the IFM can be represented as two submatrices (content and cognitive), where the number of columns of the submatrices is five (number of content features) and four (number of cognitive features). Since each item has only one content and one cognitive feature, one characteristic of each submatrix is that any one column (feature) is perfectly dependent on the other columns (features), which thus leads to rank deficiency in each submatrix. Because of double rank deficiency of the item feature incidence matrix, item feature effects (w_{kl}) at Level 3 of the IFM cannot be estimated without additional constraints, a problem analogous to a multicollinearity problem in multiple linear regression analysis.

We bypassed this problem by fixing the effects of one feature for each of the content and cognitive categories at zero (thereby also allowing the items to serve as "linking items," that is, items linking the θ metrics across countries). The relative effects of item features can be recovered once the effects are normalized across features. Figure 1 presents an illustration of the normalization procedure for the content feature effects. The shaded part of the left-hand side of the figure is the unnormalized feature effects to be estimated; the other parts of the figure are fixed at zero for model identification purposes. We then normalized these "raw" effects so that all marginal sums of the effects became zeroes, as in the right-hand side of the figure. We applied the same procedure to the cognitive feature effects. This normalization provides one way of dealing with the indeterminacy of the θ metric across groups. The estimates of μ_k, the mean of student abilities (θ) in country k, can then also be adjusted by applying the same normalizing constants to the μ_k estimates. Because the estimated μ_k's are, in many ways, of secondary importance compared to the normalized feature effect profiles, we consider their estimates only briefly in the results section.

Figure 1: Normalization procedure for content feature effects

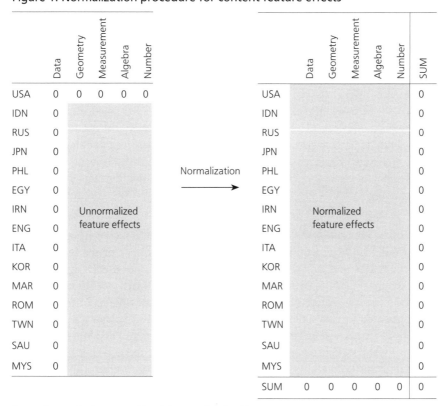

Note: Full names for the country abbreviations are given in Table 1.

DATA

Data for this study came from the TIMSS 2003 Grade 8 mathematics administration. Data were collected from 49 countries using a two-stage stratified sampling design. For each participating country, schools were sampled first, followed by random selection of a Grade 8 mathematics classroom within each participating school. All students within the sampled class were administered the test. Items were administered using a matrix sampling design involving a total of 12 possible test booklets, with each student receiving one booklet consisting of two or four mathematics item blocks. In total, 194 items were organized across the booklets. In the current study, we analyzed data from only the 15 most populated countries, and considered item responses only from the seven released blocks (99 items). Table 1 lists the 15 selected countries and their abbreviated names. We then selected from each country a random sample of 1,000 examinees administered any 10 of the 12 booklets, a process that gave a total sample size of 15,000 examinees.

Table 1: Names of the 15 most populated countries and their abbreviations

United States	USA
Indonesia	IDN
Russia	RUS
Japan	JPN
Philippines	PHL
Egypt	EGY
Iran	IRN
England	ENG
Italy	ITA
Republic of Korea	KOR
Morocco	MAR
Romania	ROM
Chinese Taipei	TWN
Saudi Arabia	SAU
Malaysia	MYS

MCMC ESTIMATION

We fitted the three-level IFM to the TIMSS dataset using a Markov chain Monte Carlo (MCMC) procedure implemented in WinBUGS (Spiegelhalter, Thomas, Best, & Lunn, 2003). This approach requires initial specification of the model and a prior for all model parameters. Using a Metropolis-Hastings algorithm, WinBUGS then attempts to simulate draws of parameter vectors derived from the joint posterior distribution of the model parameters. The success of the algorithm is evaluated by whether the chain converges to a stationary distribution, in which case characteristics of that posterior distribution (e.g., the sample mean for each parameter) can be taken as point estimates of the model parameters. In the current application, we chose the following priors for the model parameters:

$$\gamma_0 \sim N(0, 1),\ \tau_0^2 \sim \text{Inverse Gamma } (1, 1),\ \sigma_k^2 \sim \text{Inverse Gamma } (.5, .5),$$
$$\delta_{i1} \sim N(0, 10),\ w_{kl} \sim N(0, 10);$$

where γ_0 is the overall ability mean across countries, τ_0^2 is the variance of country means (μ_k), σ_k^2 is the variance of person abilities (θ_{jk}) within country k, δ_{i1} is the difficulty parameter of item i for country 1 (reference country), and w_{kl} is the random effect of country k for the feature l.

In MCMC estimation, several additional issues require consideration during monitoring of the chain's sampling history. WinBUGS, by default, uses an initial 4,000 iterations to "learn" how to generate values from proposal distributions to optimize sampling under Metropolis-Hastings. In the present analysis, we used an additional 1,000 iterations as a "burn-in" period, and simulated and inspected an additional 10,000 iterations for convergence using visual inspection as well as convergence statistics available in CODA (Best, Cowles, & Vines, 1996). We did not incorporate sampling weights in this analysis.

RESULTS

Our visual inspection of the chain histories and CODA diagnostics supported chain convergence out to 15,000 iterations. In particular, we obtained, by running five chains, the *R*-hat statistics suggested by Gelman and Rubin (1992), the values of which were all 1.0 when rounded to the first decimal, which suggests chain convergence. As a further validity check, we examined if the estimated country means (μ_k) correctly represented the known rank order of overall performance across countries based on normal scoring procedures (see, for example, Mullis et al., 2004). As described previously, we normalized the feature effects and added the corresponding normalizing constant for each country to its estimated μ_k. (This process was unnecessary for the reference country, which already had its feature effects normalized in the initial solution.) We then compared the resulting ability means for each country with the mean of the TIMSS scale scores for each country (Mullis et al., 2004, p. 34). A Pearson product-moment correlation coefficient of 0.99 and a Spearman rank-order correlation coefficient of 0.97 confirmed that we were correctly representing the mean ability levels among countries.

Tables 2 and 3 show the estimated content and cognitive feature effects, along with the posterior standard deviations (PSDs) of these for each country for the first (and primary) MCMC run. In order to compare both across features within country and across countries within feature, we calibrated the normalizing coefficients needed for this purpose at each iteration and added these to the reference country and category effects. Once these were normalized, we could compare the feature effects both within a country as well as between countries and thereby obtain profile information. For example, a look across the rows in Tables 2 and 3 allows us to evaluate the relative difficulty of different feature types for a given country, while a look down the columns allows us to determine the relative difficulty of each feature across countries. As noted, the standard deviations of feature effects across countries were estimated at each posterior simulation, and their means across simulations appear at the bottom of Tables 2 and 3. These indicate the variability of the content and cognitive feature effects across countries. From the tables we can see that the content feature effects show more variability across countries than do the cognitive feature effects. Among the content feature effects, "geometry" has the largest variability and "number" the lowest.

Table 2: Normalized effects of content features and PSDs (in parentheses)

	Number	Geometry	Measurement	Algebra	Data
USA	-0.08 (0.03)	0.43 (0.03)	0.04 (0.03)	0.02 (0.03)	-0.40 (0.04)
IDN	0.03 (0.03)	-0.07 (0.03)	0.17 (0.03)	-0.04 (0.03)	-0.08 (0.04)
RUS	0.04 (0.03)	0.06 (0.03)	-0.13 (0.03)	-0.20 (0.03)	0.23 (0.04)
JPN	0.31 (0.03)	-0.34 (0.04)	-0.03 (0.03)	0.05 (0.03)	0.01 (0.04)
PHL	-0.12 (0.03)	0.22 (0.04)	0.04 (0.04)	-0.14 (0.03)	0.00 (0.04)
EGY	-0.10 (0.03)	-0.02 (0.03)	0.22 (0.03)	-0.03 (0.03)	-0.07 (0.04)
IRN	-0.03 (0.03)	-0.25 (0.03)	0.31 (0.04)	0.04 (0.03)	-0.06 (0.04)
ENG	0.07 (0.03)	0.14 (0.03)	-0.17 (0.03)	0.22 (0.03)	-0.26 (0.04)
ITA	0.01 (0.03)	0.24 (0.03)	-0.41 (0.03)	0.10 (0.03)	0.05 (0.04)
KOR	0.00 (0.03)	-0.26 (0.04)	0.15 (0.03)	-0.18 (0.03)	0.29 (0.04)
MAR	0.03 (0.03)	-0.25 (0.03)	0.12 (0.04)	-0.02 (0.03)	0.12 (0.05)
ROM	0.07 (0.03)	0.10 (0.03)	-0.13 (0.03)	-0.16 (0.03)	0.12 (0.04)
TWN	0.07 (0.03)	0.03 (0.04)	-0.11 (0.03)	-0.11 (0.03)	0.12 (0.05)
SAU	-0.14 (0.03)	-0.17 (0.04)	0.11 (0.04)	0.24 (0.03)	-0.04 (0.05)
MYS	-0.18 (0.03)	0.15 (0.03)	-0.15 (0.03)	0.22 (0.03)	-0.04 (0.04)
SD	0.12	0.22	0.19	0.15	0.18

Table 3: Normalized effects of cognitive features and PSDs (in parentheses)

	Using concepts	Knowing facts and procedures	Solving routine problems	Reasoning
USA	0.05 (0.03)	-0.02 (0.02)	0.02 (0.02)	-0.05 (0.03)
IDN	0.07 (0.03)	-0.09 (0.03)	-0.07 (0.03)	0.09 (0.03)
RUS	0.00 (0.03)	-0.06 (0.03)	0.02 (0.02)	0.03 (0.03)
JPN	0.09 (0.03)	0.04 (0.03)	-0.13 (0.03)	0.00 (0.03)
PHL	-0.08 (0.03)	-0.08 (0.03)	0.14 (0.03)	0.02 (0.04)
EGY	0.09 (0.03)	-0.20 (0.03)	0.02 (0.03)	0.09 (0.03)
IRN	-0.06 (0.03)	0.00 (0.03)	0.03 (0.03)	0.03 (0.03)
ENG	0.08 (0.03)	0.16 (0.03)	-0.07 (0.02)	-0.18 (0.03)
ITA	0.03 (0.03)	0.21 (0.03)	-0.04 (0.02)	-0.20 (0.03)
KOR	-0.01 (0.03)	0.14 (0.03)	0.02 (0.03)	-0.15 (0.03)
MAR	-0.17 (0.03)	0.02 (0.03)	0.15 (0.03)	-0.01 (0.04)
ROM	0.02 (0.03)	-0.09 (0.03)	-0.07 (0.03)	0.14 (0.03)
TWN	0.05 (0.03)	-0.01 (0.03)	-0.19 (0.03)	0.15 (0.03)
SAU	-0.14 (0.03)	0.00 (0.03)	0.13 (0.03)	0.01 (0.04)
MYS	-0.03 (0.03)	-0.02 (0.03)	0.02 (0.02)	0.03 (0.03)
SD	0.08	0.11	0.10	0.11

One advantage of the IFM is its ability to define profiles for both countries and features. Figures 2 through 5 demonstrate how our ML-IRT model could ultimately be used to study between-country differences. Figure 2 shows the content feature effects for each of the 15 countries. The most conspicuous coefficient in the graphs is the geometry effect for the United States. We can interpret the large positive value in terms of geometry being a significant contributor to the difficulty of test items for US students relative to students from other countries; that is, geometry items demonstrate disproportionately greater difficulty for US students relative to items associated with other content features. By contrast, for a country such as Japan, geometry items demonstrate disproportionately less difficulty relative to items associated with other content features. This observation aligns with the results reported in the literature. Indeed, Tatsuoka et al. (2004) reported that US students performed poorly on geometry relative to other countries on TIMSS 1999. Mullis et al. (2004) have also reported that US students performed poorly on geometry in TIMSS 2003.

Figure 3 illustrates the normalized cognitive feature effects by country. Relative to the content feature effects, the cognitive feature effects are mostly non-significant contributors to variability in the item difficulties across countries. We can still find some significant contributors, such as the cognitive feature "knowing facts and procedures," which makes items relatively more difficult for students in Italy and makes items relatively easier for students in Egypt. As with the content feature effects, however, it is important to note that the sum to zero constraint requires that these effects always be interpreted in a relative fashion—an equivalent interpretation might emphasize the other cognitive features as relatively easier.

Figures 4 and 5 provide country effects with respect to each of the content and cognitive features. In these graphs, we can compare countries on each feature. For example, the "number" feature makes items relatively harder for Japanese students whereas it makes items relatively easier for Malaysian students. Similar interpretations can be applied for the cognitive features (Figure 5). For example, students in England, Italy, and Korea have relative strengths for "reasoning".

Figure 2: Content feature effects +/– two PSDs, by countries

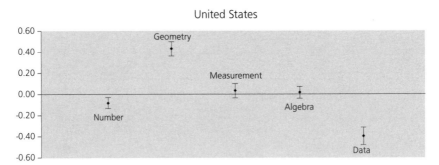

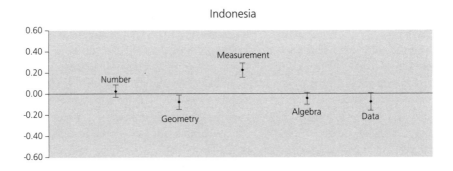

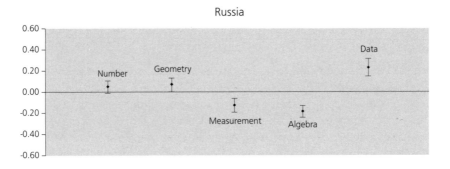

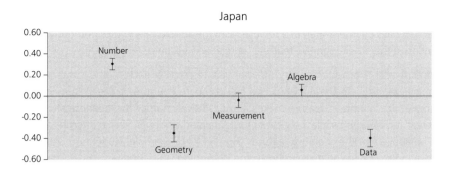

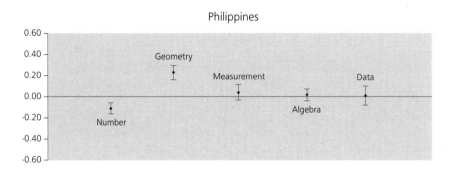

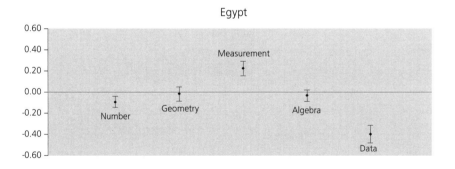

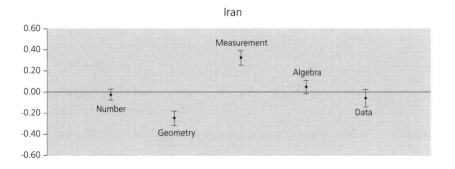

England

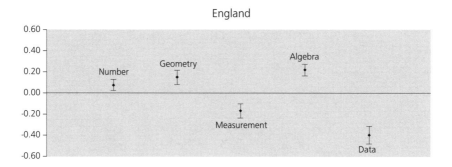

Italy

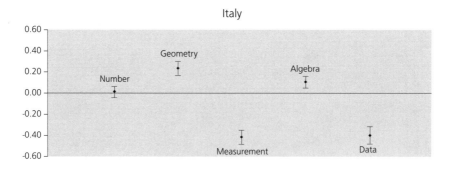

Republic of Korea

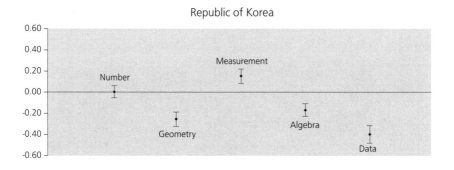

Morocco

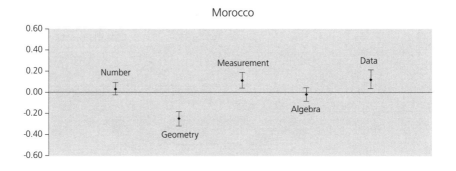

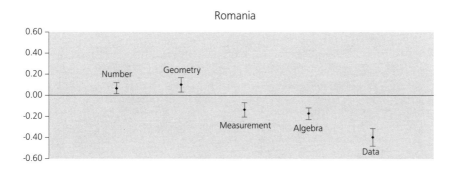

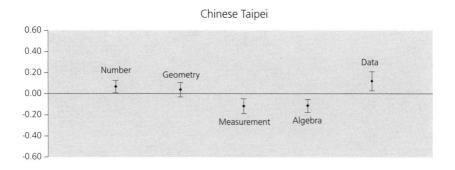

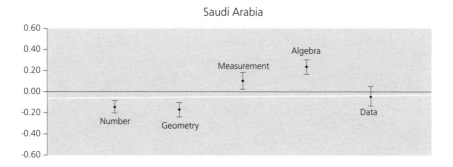

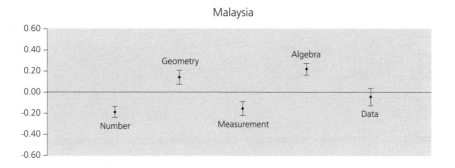

Figure 3: Cognitive feature effects +/– two PSDs, by countries

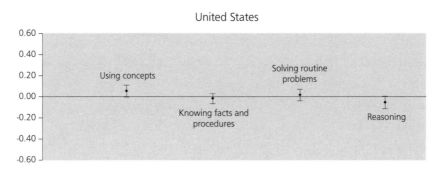

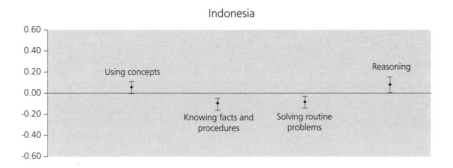

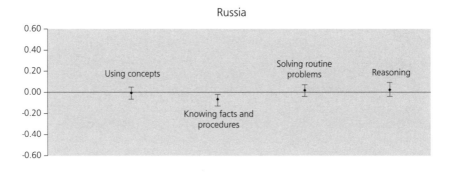

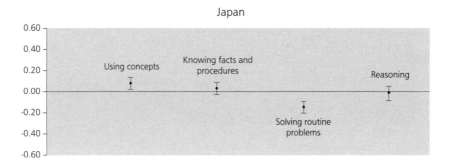

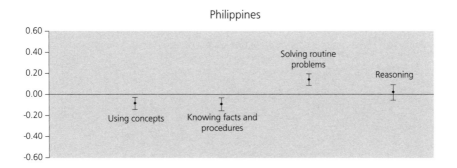

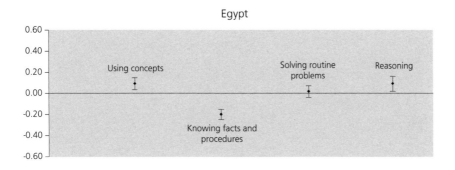

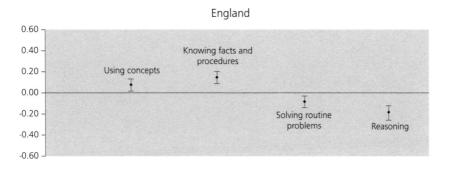

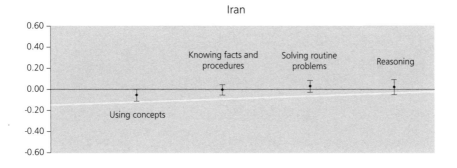

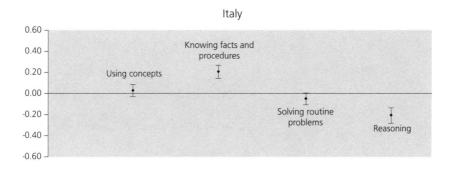

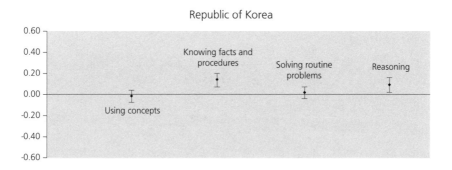

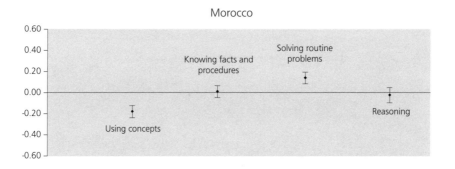

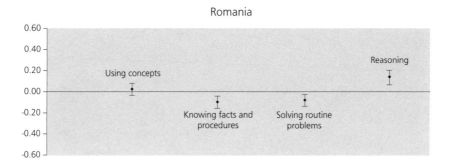

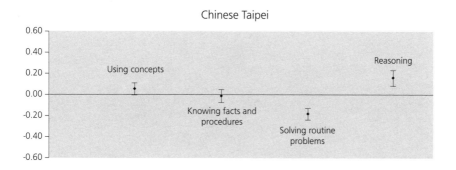

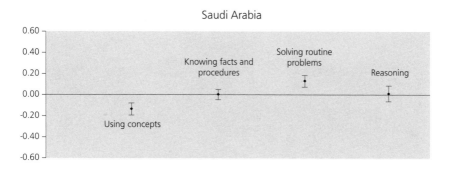

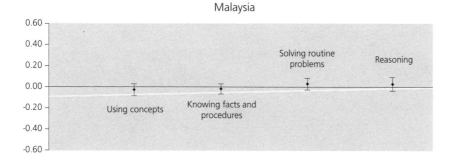

Figure 4: Country effects +/– two PSDs, by content features

Number

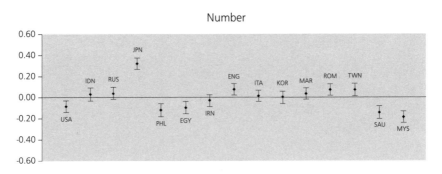

Geometry

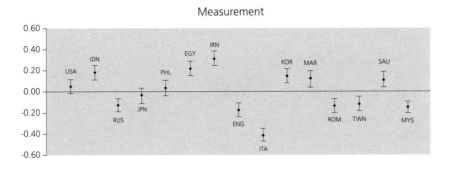

Measurement

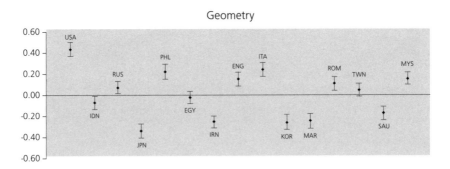

Algebra

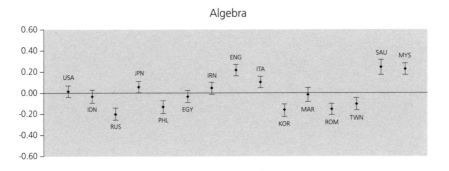

Data

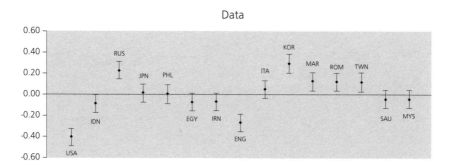

Figure 5: Country effects +/– two PSDs, by cognitive features

Using Concepts

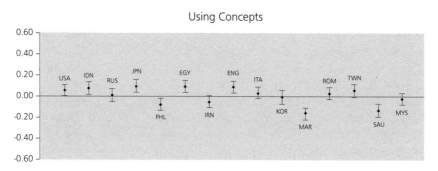

Knowing Facts and Procedures

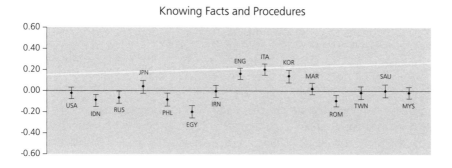

Solving Routine Problems

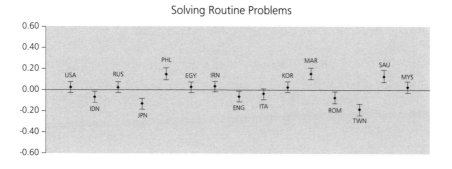

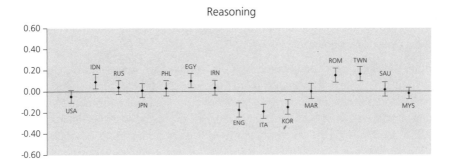

When considering Figures 2 to 5, it is important to recognize the effect of the normalization on the results being inspected and the implications this has for interpretation. Because the feature effects for each country are assumed to sum to zero, the figures illustrate only those effects related to the relative difficulty of items; in other words, the effects can be interpreted in comparison to the other feature effects within each country or to the other country effects given to each feature. The other critical component in determining the overall difficulty of the items within countries is the ability distribution within each country. As noted, our analysis estimated a mean ability for each country. It is only by considering this mean ability that we can better understand what the overall difficulties of the items are for a given country. Table 4 shows the adjusted estimates of μ's ($\hat{\mu}_{Adj}$) and the average TIMSS scale scores for each country.

DISCUSSION AND CONCLUSION

The purpose of this article was to illustrate a general methodology that could provide the foundation for diagnostic score reports at the country level based on TIMSS. As noted, the approach taken is somewhat simplistic, but it could be extended to incorporate a variety of other features that reflect greater sensitivity to the sampling design used with the assessment. Although, in the current analysis, the results seem to provide comparable results to methods already used with TIMSS, there are several potential advantages of the current methodology relative to that used for current TIMSS reports (Mullis et al., 2005). Because the methodology models how the specific domains simultaneously contribute to DIF at the group (country) level, as opposed to the current TIMSS reports, which are based on the distribution of separate proficiencies at the group level (Mullis et al., 2004, 2005), it is likely that it more effectively separates the relative effects of the cognitive and the content features. The use of DIF for diagnostic score reporting has been demonstrated in previous work (e.g., Prowker & Camilli, 2007), and it seems particularly well suited for assessments like TIMSS, where information is obtained at the group level on a large number of different items (even though relatively few are administered to individual examinees). The potential confounding of cognitive and content feature effects can be examined empirically. Cross-tabulation between content and cognitive features for the 99 items used in this analysis (Table 5) suggests the potential for dependence between content and cognitive features, although the chi-square statistic in this case was not statistically significant (χ^2_{12}, $p = 0.19$).

Another advantage of the approach is its comparative simplicity in terms of implementation. The relative standing of all countries on specific domains is made in reference to a single latent proficiency, and thus does not require the more extensive linking procedures used when modeling multiple proficiencies either separately or jointly. Indeed, one of the strengths of ML-IRT is that groups as well as individuals are all units of analysis, and thus, in similar vein to concurrent calibration, the linking procedure is incorporated within one general framework (Park, Kang, & Wollack, 2007).

Table 4: Adjusted estimates of ability means (M) and mean ability scale scores on TIMSS 2003 for each country

	$\hat{\mu}_{Adj}$	Average TIMSS scale score
KOR	0.99	589
TWN	0.93	585
JPN	0.74	570
RUS	0.07	508
ENG	-0.01	498
MYS	-0.05	508
USA	-0.07	504
ROM	-0.26	475
ITA	-0.29	484
EGY	-0.67	406
IDN	-0.96	411
IRN	-1.04	411
MAR	-1.23	387
PHL	-1.31	378
SAU	-1.60	332
Correlation	Pearson	0.99
	Spearman	0.97

Table 5: Cross-tabulation between content and cognitive features for the 99 items

Cognitive \ Content	Number	Geometry	Measurement	Algebra	Data	Sum
Using concepts	7	5	2	5	2	21
Knowing facts and procedures	8	4	7	7	0	26
Solving routine problems	14	3	6	7	4	34
Reasoning	2	4	2	5	5	18
Sum	31	16	17	24	11	99

Although we have not examined in this paper how well the specified content and cognitive features account for the DIF observed across countries, it is possible to do this with the current methodology, given that other sources of DIF (besides the item features) are undoubtedly present. One potential extension of the model considered in this article would be to add a residual to each country-specific item difficulty parameter, so as to explicitly account for the presence of other sources of country-level DIF. To get a better sense of the importance of the features in explaining DIF, we calculated simple R^2 statistics by regressing the differences of item difficulty parameter estimates between each of the comparison countries and the reference country onto the binary item features incidence matrix. The average R^2 statistic across countries was 0.166, indicating substantial other sources of DIF besides the features examined in our analysis. In other words, it would appear that the features currently emphasized in TIMSS score reporting do not go very far in explaining variability that exists between countries. Whether a better set of features exists or whether such variability is simply due to item-specific characteristics remains an important direction for future exploration.

It is necessary to acknowledge a number of limitations of the current analysis, and crucial other directions for future work. As noted, our analysis was not sensitive to the sampling weights present in the TIMSS design. In addition, it ignored other levels (e.g., school) that could be added using the same modeling framework. Also, because the analysis was based on only the 99 released items from the TIMSS assessment and included only the 15 countries with the largest samples, it should be extended to include the full 194 items and more countries. Larger samples may also help in estimating certain parameters of the model, such as the trait variances and country weights, which tend to be more challenging to estimate accurately. Other aspects of the analysis, such as our use of dichotomous scoring for items that were polytomously scored, could be relaxed so that the full range of item scores is considered. Finally, steps can also be taken to improve the estimation of the model. The MCMC run for the analysis presented in this article took more than a day, even on a relatively fast machine.

Although distinct from the Tatsuoka et al. (2004) rule-space approach, the current methodology could also accommodate more specific codings of items, such as those used in rule-space applications to TIMSS. As noted, Tatsuoka et al. (2004) identified 23 content and cognitive skill attributes in the TIMSS Grade 8 mathematics assessment in 1999. Since those attributes were found to explain most of the variation in item difficulties, the same attributes may be applied to account more fully for DIF observed across countries.

This research was supported by a grant to the first author from the American Educational Research Association, which receives funds for its "AERA Grants Program" from the National Science Foundation and the National Center for Education Statistics of the Institute of Education Sciences (U.S. Department of Education) under NSF Grant #REC-0310268. Opinions reflect those of the authors and do not necessarily reflect those of the granting agencies.

References

Adams, R. J., Wilson, M., & Wu, M. (1997). Multilevel item response models: An approach to errors in variables regression. *Journal of Educational and Behavioral Statistics, 22*, 47–76.

Best, N., Cowles, M. K., & Vines, K. (1996). *CODA*: Convergence Diagnosis and Output Analysis Software for Gibbs Sampling Output, Version 0.30*. Cambridge, UK: MRC Biostatistics Unit..

Cheong, Y. F., & Raudenbush, S. W. (2000). Measurement and structural models for children's problem behaviors. *Psychological Methods, 5*, 477–495.

De Boeck, P., & Wilson, M. (Eds.) (2004). *Explanatory item response models*. New York, NY: Springer.

Embretson, S. E., & Reise, S. P. (2000). *Item response theory for psychologists*. Mahwah, NJ: Lawrence Erlbaum.

Fox, J.-P. (2003). Stochastic EM for estimating the parameters of a multilevel IRT model. *British Journal of Mathematical and Statistical Psychology, 56*, 65–81.

Fox, J.-P., & Glas, C. A. W. (2001). Bayesian estimation of a multilevel IRT model using Gibbs sampling. *Psychometrika, 66*, 271–288.

Gelman, A., & Rubin, D. B. (1992). Inference from iterative simulation using multiple sequences. *Statistical Science, 7*, 457–472.

Haberman, S. J., & von Davier, M. (2007). Some notes on models for cognitively-based skills diagnosis. In C. R. Rao & S. Sinharay (Eds.), *Handbook of statistics: Vol. 26. Psychometrics* (pp. 1031–1038). Amsterdam: Elsevier.

Hambleton, R. K., & Swaminathan, H. (1985). *Item response theory: Principles and applications*. Boston, MA: Kluwer.

Kamata, A. (2001). Item analysis by the hierarchical generalized linear model. *Journal of Educational Measurement, 38*, 79–93.

Kamata, A. (2002, April). *Procedure to perform item response analysis by hierarchical generalized linear model*. Paper presented at the 2002 annual meeting of the American Educational Research Association, New Orleans, LA.

McCulloch, C. E., & Searle, S. R. (2001). *Generalized, linear, and mixed models*. New York, NY: Wiley.

Mullis, I. V. S., Martin, M. O., & Foy, P. (2005). *IEA's TIMSS 2003 international report on achievement in the mathematics cognitive domains*. Chestnut Hill, MA: Boston College.

Mullis, I. V. S., Martin, M. O., Gonzalez, E. J., & Chrostowski, S. J. (2004). *TIMSS 2003 international mathematics report*. Chestnut Hill, MA: Boston College.

Park, C., Kang, T., & Wollack, J. A. (2007, April). *Application of multilevel IRT to multiple-form linking when common items are drifted*. Paper presented at the 2007 annual meeting of the National Council on Measurement in Education, Chicago, IL.

Prowker, A., & Camilli, G. (2007). Looking beyond the overall scores of NAEP assessments: Applications of generalized linear mixed modeling for exploring value-added item difficulty effects. *Journal of Educational Measurement, 44*, 69–87.

Raudenbush, S. W., & Bryk, A. S. (2002). *Hierarchical linear models* (2nd ed.). Thousand Oaks, CA: Sage.

Rijmen, F., Tuerlinckx, F., De Boeck, P., & Kuppens, P. (2003). A nonlinear mixed model framework for item response theory. *Psychological Methods, 8*(2), 185–205.

Spiegelhalter, D. J., Thomas A., Best, N. G., & Lunn, D. (2003). *WinBUGS Version 1.4 user manual*. Cambridge, England: MRC Biostatistics Unit.

Tatsuoka, K. K., Corter, J. E., & Tatsuoka, C. (2004). Patterns of diagnosed mathematical content and process skills in TIMSS-R across a sample of 20 countries. *American Educational Research Journal, 41*, 901–926.

von Davier, M., Sinharay, S., Oranje, A., & Beaton, A. (2007). The statistical procedures used in National Assessment of Educational Progress: Recent developments and future directions. In C. R. Rao & S. Sinharay (Eds.), *Handbook of statistics: Vol. 26. Psychometrics* (pp. 1039–1055). North Holland: Elsevier.

Linking for the general diagnostic model

Xueli Xu and Matthias von Davier
Educational Testing Service, Princeton, New Jersey, United States

This study analyzed National Assessment of Educational Progress (NAEP) reading data using a general diagnostic model (GDM) in order to investigate and compare three strategies for linking two consecutive assessments. These strategies are compared in terms of marginal and joint expectations of skills, joint probabilities of skill patterns, and item parameter estimates. The results indicate that fixing item parameter values at their previously calibrated values is sufficient to establish a comparable scale for the subsequent year.

INTRODUCTION

Cognitive diagnosis models (DiBello, Stout, & Roussos, 1995; Junker & Sijtsma, 2000; Maris, 1999; Tatsuoka, 1983; von Davier 2005; von Davier & Rost, 2006) have been developed for in-depth analysis of item response data. In such models, the latent abilities or skill profiles are represented by a discrete set of real valued numbers. For example, one can specify $\{0, 1\}$ for skill spaces with mastery/non-mastery status or $\{-4.0, -3.8, -3.6, ..., +3.6, +3.8, +4.0\}$ for skill spaces with more than two levels that emulate unidimensional item response theory (IRT) models. The non-continuous nature of the skill profiles makes the linking across assessments non-trivial. It is appropriate to use a linking strategy in IRT models based on linear transformations when the ability distribution is assumed to follow a standard normal distribution. However, the linear linking approach might not be appropriate for discrete latent skills. Our primary goal in this article is to compare three proposed linking strategies with respect to various aspects by using a general diagnostic model (GDM) containing discrete skill profiles. The article is organized as follows. Section 1 gives a brief introduction to GDMs in general and the model used in our study in particular. In Section 2, we introduce three proposed linking strategies. Section 3 outlines our evaluation criteria, the data we drew on, and our results, including the results of analyses we conducted relative to key subgroups from our datasets. In Section 4, we complete the article by presenting a brief discussion and conclusion.

GENERAL DIAGNOSTIC MODELS

The general diagnostic model or GDM (von Davier, 2005) is a framework that allows researchers to integrate approaches involving confirmatory multidimensional models with discrete latent trait variables. Within the GDM framework, the flexible form of the functioning of skills (cognitive attributes) allows specification of many well-known psychometric models, such as IRT models (Lord & Novick, 1968), the fusion model (DiBello et al., 1995; Hartz, 2002), and various IRT models (for an overview, see von Davier & Rost, 2006).

The special form of the GDM that we use in our study, suitable for dichotomous and partial credit data, is represented by the following equation:

$$P(X=x \mid \beta_i, \alpha, q_i, \gamma_i) = \frac{\exp \left[\beta_{xi} + x \sum_{k=1}^{K} \gamma_{ik} q_{ik} \alpha_k \right]}{1 + \sum_{y=1}^{mi} \exp \left[\beta_{yi} + y \sum_{k1} \gamma_{ik} q_{ik} \alpha_k \right]}$$

In this equation, q_{ik} is an entry of the Q-matrix, which specifies the correspondence between item i and skill k. If skill k is required to solve item i, then $q_{ik}=1$; otherwise, $q_{ik}=0$. The total number of skills is denoted by K. Content experts prespecify the Q-matrix, which represents a hypothesis about the relationship between students' skills and students' item responses. Thus, in the above equation, y is an index for possible scores for item i, and m_i denotes the maximum score for this item. According to the equation (1), the probability of obtaining score x on item i depends on the item parameters $\beta_{xi}, \beta_{yi}, \gamma_{ik}$ and on the student skill profile α_k. In this model, the values α_k's take on α_k a finite set of real valued numbers that the user sets in his or her model specification.

Similar to IRT models, GDMs require that certain conditions are met to remove the indeterminacy of the scale. Different methods can be used to determine the scale. Thus, for example, $\beta_{11}=0$ can be fixed to a certain constant and some or all slopes set to fixed constants. For example, γ_{11} and γ_{1k} for $K>1$, or the mean of the difficulties as well as the (log)-average of the slopes are set to constant values. Alternatively, in models with several ability levels, the mean and variance of the ability variables can be fixed to certain values, much like the commonly used assumption of a standard normal distribution in IRT models.

LINKING STRATEGIES

Trend maintenance is an important concept in most large-scale assessments with multiple cycles. A considerable portion of items is common across two consecutive assessments designed to establish or continue the trend. In the remainder of this article, we denote these two consecutive assessments via Y1 and Y2, set in chronological order. Because we assumed that the scale of Y1 was established from a previous calibration before consideration was given to the linkage between Y1 and Y2, we denote this previous calibration of Y1 as Y1 *calibration* throughout this article.

A *concurrent* calibration strategy is used in the operational linking analysis of National Assessment of Educational Progress (NAEP) data (Mislevy, 1992; Muraki & Hombo, 1999). The strategy includes three steps that endeavor to build a linkage between the *Y1 calibration* and the *Y2*. The first step involves establishing a common scale for *Y1* and *Y2* through a concurrent calibration of the data from *Y1* and *Y2*, and setting common items to have the same item parameter estimates. This step makes it possible to obtain the mean and variance of the latent ability for students in *Y1* and *Y2* in the concurrent calibration. The second step is to form a bridge between the *Y1 calibration* and the concurrent calibration by finding a linear transformation that makes the mean and the variance of the latent ability for students in *Y1* from both calibrations equal to each other. Finally, the third step involves establishing the link between the *Y1 calibration* and the *Y2* by applying this linear transformation to *Y2* from the concurrent calibration.

This concurrent calibration strategy is valid when the latent ability is assumed to follow a normal distribution. The reason for this is that, with normal distributions, any two distributions can be perfectly matched by a location and scale transformation. This is not true, however, for more general distributions, such as those that require full specification of three or more parameters. In addition, as Haberman (2005) has shown, attempts to use two-parameter-logistic (2PL) and three-parameter-logistic (3PL) models with ability distributions that are more general in nature than the standard normal distribution require careful work. Specifically, the linear transformation in Steps 2 and 3 is not appropriate for discrete latent variables. For example, if the latent skill is prespecified to have six real-valued levels {-2, -1, -0.5, 0.5, 1, 2}, any linear transformations other than identity (slope=1, and intercept=0) and negative identity (slope=-1, and intercept=0) are not valid. A linear transformation with slope=2 and intercept=0 leads to a set of {-4,-2,-1, 1, 2, 4}, which is out of the range of the original set of α_k. So, in developing the linking strategy under discrete latent trait models, we have to use methods that avoid the need for linear transformations. The three strategies that we consider in this article are all based on the concurrent calibration described above. Strategy 2 is actually the first step of the concurrent calibration linking. Although Strategy 2 cannot establish a good link because Steps 2 and 3 are missing, we have included it for comparison with Strategy 1. We consider Strategy 1 to be more stringent than Strategy 2 because the parameter estimates for the common items are fixed, like those in the *Y1 calibration*. Strategy 3 also relies on a strong assumption regarding the role of the common items. Our hypothesis therefore is that the common items will be sufficient to build a link between the *Y1 calibration* and the *Y2*. Moreover, although we knew it was likely that Strategies 1 and 3 would be the same when no constraints were imposed on item parameters, we recognized that certain constraints must be imposed in many situations involving GDMs in order to make the models identifiable. While in our case these constraints would make Strategies 1 and 3 different, we suspected that the differences in most cases would be small.

The details of our three linking strategies follow:

- *Linking Strategy 1:* Under this strategy, *Y1* and *Y2* are calibrated concurrently, with the common items fixed at the values obtained from the *Y1 calibration*. This calibration does not reestimate the item parameters of the common items for *Y2* but rather assumes the parameters of these items are fixed at known values. In addition, items not common to *Y1* and *Y2* are reestimated in a joint calibration with unique sets of parameters for each of the years.

- *Linking Strategy 2:* This strategy calibrates *Y1* and *Y2* concurrently, with the common items set to be equal across (for this study) two years. This procedure involves reestimating all item parameters in a joint calibration, while assuming that the parameters of items common to *Y1* and Y2 are equal and do not change over assessment cycles.

- *Linking Strategy 3:* This strategy establishes the link by calibrating the *Y2* assessment data separately, with common items fixed at the values obtained from the *Y1 calibration*.

EVALUATION CRITERIA

Before presenting our analysis, we briefly outline the criteria that we used to evaluate the different strategies. Within an IRT modeling framework, a good recovery of the basic characteristics of *Y1* is often used as the criterion for a good linking. For example, in a concurrent calibration, the rationale behind Steps 2 and 3 is to make sure that the characteristics of *Y1* stay the same from the *Y1 calibration* to the concurrent calibration. If we assume a normal distribution for the latent ability in the IRT models, then the mean and the variance are sufficient to maintain the shape of the latent ability. However, the mean and variance are no longer sufficient for a discrete latent skill distribution. Thus, when we estimate multidimensional skills simultaneously, we should estimate the joint probabilities so as to describe the characteristics of the latent skill distributions. Accordingly, in this study, we also report, in addition to the joint probability distributions, the joint expectation of latent skills and the marginal probability of skills for key subgroups as the criteria by which to evaluate the three different linking strategies.

DATA

The data that we used to compare the three linking strategies were drawn from two NAEP Grade 4 reading assessments. Our first dataset contained a subset of the 2003 assessment data, and our second dataset was a subset of the 2005 assessment. The dataset from 2003 contained 47,817 students' responses to 102 items under a partially balanced incomplete block (pBIB) design from two subscales ($K=2$): reading for literary experience and reading to gain information. The 2005 dataset included 41,420 students' responses to 99 items under the pBIB design employing the same two subscales. The two assessments had 69 items in common. The data from 2003 served as the *Y1* data, while the data from 2005 served as the *Y2* data.

ANALYSIS

In the reading framework, each item from both the *Y1* and the *Y2* data is assigned to one of the two reading subscales—reading for literary experience and reading for information. The correspondence between items and subscales defined in the framework served as our Q-matrix. This setting is equivalent to a two-dimensional IRT model that has a simple structure represented by the allocation of each item to only one of the subscales. Because model comparisons were not a focus of our linking study, we considered no other alternative Q-matrices in relation to it. Our primary goal relative to the comparison between Strategies 1 and 2 was to determine if Strategy 1 could reproduce the scale set by the *Y1 calibration*. We considered that if Strategy 1 outperformed Strategy 2, then the comparison between Strategies 1 and 3 would allow us to determine if the release of concurrent calibration in Strategy 3 would allow us to recover the *Y1* characters.

RESULTS

The results are organized as follows: comparison between Strategies 1 and 2; comparison between the three strategies; and comparisons in terms of key subgroup statistics.

Comparison 1: Strategy 1 versus Strategy 2

The comparisons in this section are based on using fit statistics, the joint probabilities of skill patterns, and the joint and marginal expectations of skills. The fit statistics that we used in this study included the log-likelihood and the Akaike Information Criterion or AIC (Akaike, 1974) index. The AIC is defined as $-2\ln(L) + 2p$, where $\ln(L)$ is the log-likelihood of the data under the model and p is the number of parameters in the model. For a given dataset, the larger the log-likelihood, the better the model fit, and the smaller the AIC value, the better the model fit.

Table 1 gives information on our model's fit statistics. Note that the number of parameters in the table is much smaller for Strategy 1 than for Strategy 2. This is because the parameters for the common items were fixed given that they were already known from the 2003 separate calibration. Therefore, we can argue that the *actual* count of parameters is unknown for this model because it involves the 2003 data, which were separately used to determine the common item parameters in this strategy. Nevertheless, a comparison solely in terms of likelihood indicates that the differences between the two strategies were not huge for these calibrations.

Table 1: Model fit comparisons for Strategies 1 and 2

Linking	Model parameters	Log-likelihood	AIC
Strategy 1	165	-994579.93	1989469
Strategy 2	321	-993799.31	1988200

Figure 1 compares the estimated joint probabilities of skill patterns for the 2003 data (*Y1*) obtained from using Strategies 1 and 2 with those obtained from the separate calibration of 2003 (the *Y1 calibration*). If a common scale had been maintained across calibrations, we would expect all the estimated joint probabilities within the figure to be very close to one another. Within each plot of the figure, the x-axis stands for the estimated joint probability of skill patterns for the 2003 sample from the *Y1 calibration*, while the y-axis represents the corresponding probability from using either Strategy 1 or Strategy 2. The left-hand panel gives the contrast between the separate calibration and Strategy 1, while the right-hand panel gives the contrast between separate calibration and Strategy 2.

Figure 2 shows the estimated joint expectation of skills for the 2003 students under Strategies 1 and 2 against those from the *Y1 calibration*. Here, the expectation is calculated by E ($\alpha_1\alpha_2 \mid v_j$ for each person v_j, and so we could expect the estimates for the same students from the different methods to be very close to one another if a common scale had been maintained. Again, within each plot, the x-axis stands for the estimated joint expectation for the 2003 sample from the *Y1 calibration*, while the y-axis represents the corresponding expectation from using either Strategy 1 or Strategy 2.

Figure 3 presents the differences in marginal skill expectations for the 2003 students in the form of boxplots. Specifically, the left-hand graph shows the difference between the *Y1 calibration* and the use of Strategy 1, while the right-hand graph represents the difference between the *Y1 calibration* and the use of Strategy 2. The numbers 1 and 2 alongside the x-axis in each graph represent the two reading subscales, and we used $E(\alpha_k \mid v_j)$ to calculate the marginal expectation for skill k for each person v_j.

Figure 1: Joint probability comparison for the 2003 data

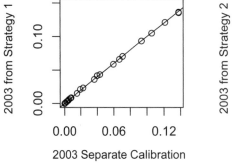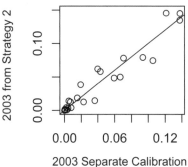

Figure 2: Joint expectation comparison for the 2003 data

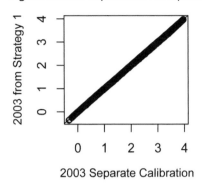
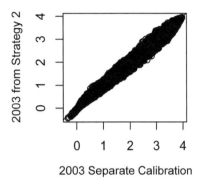

Figure 3: Marginal expectation comparison for the 2003 data

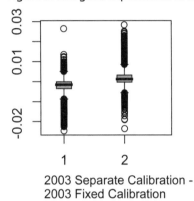
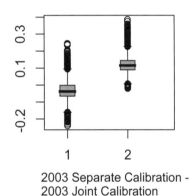

We can see from Figures 1 to 3 that the deviations from the *Y1 calibration* in terms of various statistics were smaller when we used Strategy 1 as compared to Strategy 2. Even though concurrent calibration (Strategy 2) produced a common scale for Years 2003 and 2005, it may not have produced the same scale as that established from the *Y1 calibration*. Compared to Strategy 2, Strategy 1 utilized a stronger link to connect these two consecutive assessments by using concurrent calibration coupled with fixed common-item parameter values. Therefore, Strategy 1 showed much smaller deviations from the *Y1 calibration* than did Strategy 2.

We could argue that these results would not have held if there had been fewer common items between the two tests. To answer this consideration, we investigated a case in which only 25 items were common to the two years. We randomly selected these 25 items from the original 69 common items. Table 2 gives the model-fit information for these analyses. Again, due to the fixing of item parameters in Strategy 1, the number of parameters shown in Table 2 for Strategy 1 is not accurate. Nevertheless, the difference between AIC is not large for the two strategies.

Table 2: Model fits of Strategies 1 and 2 with only 25 common items

Linking	Model parameters	Log-likelihood	AIC
Strategy 1	369	-993761.63	1988215
Strategy 2	424	-993408.44	1987612

Figures 4 to 6 show the same configuration of results as that shown in Figures 1 to 3, but this time the results relate to the 25-common-items case. The fact that the three figures present results similar to those in Figures 1 to 3 indicates that the scale established by Strategy 1 remained robust even when fewer common items were present.

Figure 4: Joint probability comparison with 25 common items from the 2003 assessment

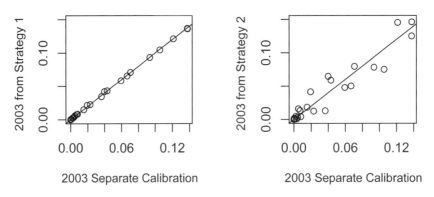

Figure 5: Joint expectation comparison with 25 common items from the 2003 assessment

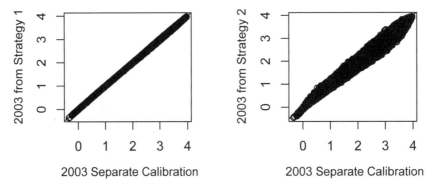

Figure 6: Marginal expectation comparison with 25 common items from the 2003 assessment

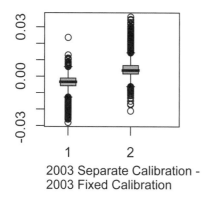

2003 Separate Calibration -
2003 Fixed Calibration

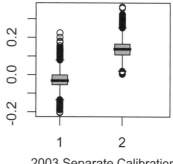

2003 Separate Calibration -
2003 Joint Calibration

Comparison 2: Three Strategies

Our intention with the comparisons set out in this section was to determine if we could establish the link between the two assessment years by dropping the concurrent calibration and using only fixed-item parameters for the subsequent calibrations. This required us to apply the common-item parameters obtained from the *Y1 calibration* directly to the analysis of the 2005 data. We conducted the comparison by using joint skill probabilities and marginal skill expectations. We also conducted our comparisons with either the 69 items or the 25 items held in common between the two tests.

The difference in the joint probabilities of skill patterns between the 2005 students and the 2003 students under the three different strategies is shown in Figure 7 in the form of boxplots. The numbers along the x-axis in Figure 7 stand for strategy ID (i.e., Strategies 1, 2, or 3). If a scale identical to that from the 2003 separate calibration had been set up by Strategy 3, then the boxplots for Strategy 1 and Strategy 3 depicted in the figure should be similar to each other. However, if the scale had not been identical, then the boxplots that we see in the figure for Strategies 1 and 2 should be similar to each other. Our analysis produced the former result, and we also obtained a similar result with the 25 common-items configuration, as shown in Figure 8.

Figures 9 and 10 show, again via boxplots, comparisons of the marginal skill expectations obtained from Strategies 2 and 3 with those from Strategy 1. In each graph, the numbers 1 and 2 along the x-axis stand for the two subscales measured in reading. The left-hand graph presents the difference between Strategies 3 and 1, while the right-hand panel illustrates the difference between Strategies 2 and 1. If an identical scale had been established through fixing the item parameter values, and not by concurrent calibration, then we could assume that the difference between Strategies 1 and 3 would be smaller than the difference between Strategies 1 and 2. The results shown in the figures confirm this, since the boxplots for both reading subscales shown in the left-hand graph are considerably more concentrated around 0 than are those in the right-hand graph.

Figure 7: Joint probability comparison: 2005 minus 2003

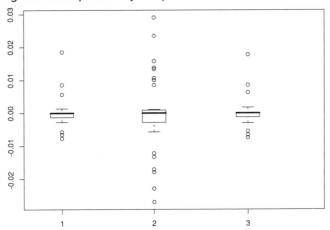

Figure 8: Joint probability comparison: 2005 minus 2003 with 25 common items

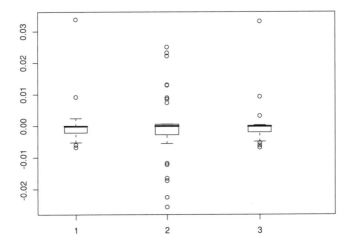

Figure 9: Marginal expectation comparison for 2005 data

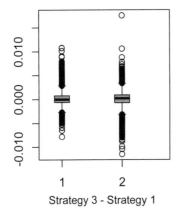

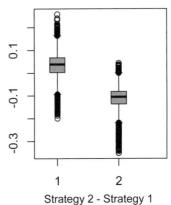

Strategy 3 - Strategy 1

Strategy 2 - Strategy 1

Figure 10: Marginal expectation comparison for 2005 data with the 25 common items

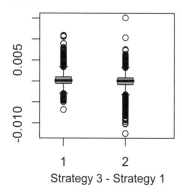
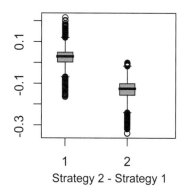

In summary, the comparisons in this section indicate that it *is* possible to reproduce in the 2005 separate calibration a scale identical to the 2003 separate calibration by fixing the common item parameters at the estimates obtained from the 2003 separate calibration.

Key Subgroups Comparison

Because it is important, relative to operational NAEP reporting purposes, to consider statistics relating to key subgroups, such as the mean, standard deviation, and quantiles, we decided to consider the skills distributions for the subgroups within the cognitive diagnosis framework that had an equivalent aggregation level. More specifically, we compared the skill distributions of several key subgroups (race/ethnicity and gender) in the 2005 assessment across linking strategies. We also compared the skill profiles of key subgroups in the 2003 assessment across strategies and with those obtained from the separate calibration of 2003. Given that the results of the case with 25 common items and the case with 69 common items were again similar to each other, we report only the results of the case with 25 common items.

In the following comparisons, we derived the skill profiles for subgroups on the basis of a single-group assumption. This means that we set all subgroups to have the same prior distribution for the latent classes. We then calculated the skill profile for a subgroup by taking a weighted average of the skill profiles of students in the subgroup; here, the weights were the student weights used in the NAEP operational analysis.

We compared the skill profiles for subgroups from the 2003 assessment between the *Y1 calibration* and Strategies 1 and 2. Figures 11 and 12 show the differences in estimated marginal skill distributions. In each graph, the subgroups are represented by a capitalized initial letter. Thus, A, B, F, H, M, and W stand for Asian, Black, Female, Hispanic, Male, and White student groups. Although we might consider the differences between the *Y1 calibration* and Strategy 2 shown in Figure 12 to be small (within a range of -0.04–0.04), the differences between the *Y1 calibration* and

Strategy 1 (shown in Figure 11) are much smaller. Thus, Strategy 1 leads to an almost identical scale to the scale from the *Y1 calibration*.

Figure 11: Differences in marginal skill profile: Separate versus Strategy 1 (2003 data)

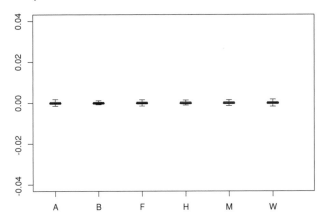

Figure 12: Differences in marginal skill profile: Separate versus Strategy 2 (2003 data)

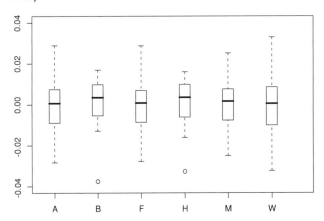

Figures 13 and 14 show the results of our comparison (between Strategy 3 and Strategies 1 and 2) of the skill profiles for the subgroups from the 2005 assessment. From these figures, we can see that Strategy 1 is much closer to Strategy 3 than it is to Strategy 2 in terms of the estimated marginal skill profile for the key subgroups. This outcome suggests that, in the case of linking these two NAEP assessments under the GDM framework, it is possible to set and reproduce a scale by fixing the values of the common items in the two assessments, even when they hold only 25 (approximately 25% of the entire test) items in common.

Figure 13: Differences in the marginal skill profile: Strategy 3 versus Strategy 1 (2005 data)

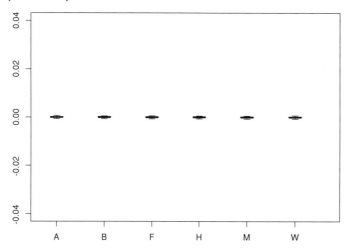

Figure 14: Differences in the marginal skill profile: Strategy 3 versus Strategy 2 (2005 data)

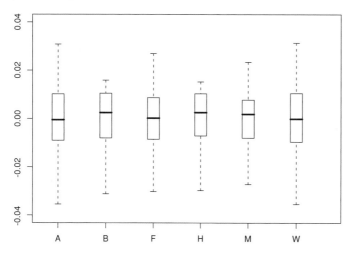

DISCUSSION AND CONCLUSION

Although the non-continuous nature of the skill locations in the GDM limits searches for appropriate linking methods, the research question that needs to be answered is what leads to a scale that is maintained across assessments and links to the scale of the *Y1 calibration*. Certainly, the bridge between target (*Y2*) and baseline year (*Y1*) is built through common items, but the nature and extent of the necessary constraints are not self-evident. We therefore compared three different strategies in this study. As previously mentioned, these three strategies are variations from the concurrent calibration linking used in NAEP operations. Often, a concurrent calibration linking consists of three steps of calibration and transformation, and Strategy 2 in this present study was indeed the first step of the concurrent calibration linking, especially given the need to intentionally drop the other steps due to their inappropriateness for discrete latent skills/abilities.

Strategy 1 produced a stronger link than Strategy 2 by fixing the common items parameters at known values from the *Y1 calibration* in addition to the concurrent calibration. With Strategy 3—a simplified version of Strategy 1—we dropped the concurrent calibration and kept the common-item parameters from the *Y1 calibration* fixed at known values. In fact, Strategy 3 would have been identical to Strategy 1 if no constraint had been imposed on the item parameter estimation procedure. Even when we did place certain constraints on the estimation process, we observed only slight differences for Strategies 1 and 3, as shown in Figures 7 to 10 and Figure 13.

All the results in our study empirically demonstrated that one linking strategy—the concurrent calibration of two adjacent assessments—is not necessary when the common items are fixed at the values obtained from the *Y1 calibration*. These similar results even held up in the case where common items consisted of only 25% of the whole NAEP assessment. Generalizing this result is not advised, however, because it may not hold up in studies with different procedures for assessment development, block formation, item flagging, and selection for subsequent assessment.

To make sure the conclusion remained true for the case where only 25 items were held in common across both tests, we carried out two additional analyses based on different sets of 25 items, and obtained similar results to those shown in this current article. We also analyzed data from a Grade 8 NAEP reading assessment in 2003 and 2005, and again drew similar conclusions from these analyses. Although the purpose of our study was not focused on model comparisons, we have to mention one special model case where only two levels (mastery and non-mastery) were specified for each cognitive skill. On running such cases, we found that the concurrent calibration of 2003 and 2005 assessments was able, as in Strategy 2, to reproduce the scale established by the *Y1 calibration*.

As discussed earlier in this article, we conducted our analysis on the basis of a single-group assumption, that is, a one-skill distribution. In our future work, we intend to undertake an analysis based on a multiple-group assumption coupled with Strategy 3. Under this assumption, we will assign the subgroups unique and potentially different prior distributions so that the skill profiles for these subgroups can be directly calculated by rerunning the software. An initial investigation of applying GDM to NAEP data (Xu & von Davier, 2006) showed that the multiple-group analysis yielded results for the racial subgroups and gender subgroups that were similar to those from the NAEP operational analyses. Our future work will also endeavor to answer additional questions, such as whether our employment of a GDM multiple-group analysis procedure will see Strategy 3 leading to a comparable scale.

References

Akaike, H. (1974). A new look at the statistical model identification. *IEEE Transactions on Automatic Control, 19*(6), 716–723.

DiBello, L. V., Stout, W. F., & Roussos, L. A. (1995). Unified cognitive/psychometric diagnostic assessment likelihood-based classification techniques. In P. D. Nichols, S. F. Chipman, & R. L. Brennan, (Eds.), *Cognitively diagnostic assessment* (pp. 361–389). Hillsdale, NJ: Lawrence Erlbaum Associates.

Haberman, S. (2005). *Identifiability of parameters in item response models with unconstrained ability distributions* (ETS Research Report Series RR-05-24). Princeton, NJ: Educational Testing Service.

Hartz, S. M. (2002). *A Bayesian framework for the unified model for assessing cognitive abilities: Blending theory with practicality*. Unpublished doctoral dissertation, University of Illinois, Champaign, IL.

Junker, B., & Sijtsma, K. (2000). Latent and manifest monotonicity in item response models. *Applied Psychological Measurement, 24*, 65–81.

Lord, F. M., & Novick, M. R. (1968). *Statistical theories of mental test scores*. Reading, MA: Addison-Wesley.

Maris, E. (1999). Estimating multiple classification latent class models. *Psychometrika, 64*(2), 187–212.

Mislevy, R. J. (1992). Scaling procedures. In E. G. Johonson & N. L. Allen (Eds.), *The NAEP 1990 technical report* (Report No. 21-TR-20, pp. 199–213). Washington DC: National Center for Education Statistics.

Muraki, E. & Hombo, C. (1999). *Application of a multiple-group generalized partial credit model to NAEP linking procedures*. Unpublished manuscript. Princeton, NJ: Educational Testing Service.

Tatsuoka, K. K. (1983). Rule space: An approach for dealing with misconceptions based on item response theory. *Journal of Educational Measurement, 20*, 345–354.

von Davier, M. (2005). *A general diagnostic model applied to language testing data* (ETS Research Report Series RR-05-16). Princeton, NJ: Educational Testing Service.

von Davier, M. & Rost, J. (2006). Mixture distribution item response models. In C. R. Rao & S. Sinharay (Eds.), *Handbook of statistics: Vol. 27. Psychometrics* (pp. 643–661). Amsterdam: Elsevier.

Xu, X., & von Davier, M. (2006). *Cognitive diagnosis for NAEP proficiency data* (ETS Research Report Series, RR-06-08). Princeton, NJ: Educational Testing Service.

Linking errors in trend estimation for international surveys in education

C. Monseur
University of Liège, Liège, Belgium

H. Sibberns and D. Hastedt
IEA Data Processing and Research Center, Hamburg, Germany

For a decade, more or less, one of the major objectives of international surveys in education has been to report trends in achievement. For that purpose, a subset of items from previous data collections has been included in new assessment instruments. The linking process (i.e., reporting the cognitive data from different data collections on a single scale) is implemented through item response theory (IRT) models. Under IRT assumptions, the same linking function is obtained regardless of which common items are used because item-specific properties are fully accounted for by the item's IRT parameters. However, model misspecifications always occur, such as small changes in the items, position effects, and curriculum effects. Therefore, other sets of linked items can generate other linking transformations, even with very large examinee samples. According to Michaelides and Haertel (2004), error due to the common-item sampling does not depend on the size of the examinee sample, but rather on the number of common items used. As such, the selection of anchor items may constitute the dominant source of error for summary scores. During its history, the International Association for the Evaluation of Educational Achievement (IEA) has reported trends in achievement for TIMSS 1999, TIMSS 2003, and PIRLS 2001, but has not accounted for linking errors in addition to the usual sampling and imputation errors, a situation that leads to an increase in Type I errors. It is for this reason that this study analyzes the variability of the trends estimate due to the selection and length of the anchor test used to link the assessments.

INTRODUCTION

The interest taken by policy-makers in monitoring education systems and measuring the effects of educational reforms has contributed to an increased emphasis on trend indicators in the design of recent surveys of educational achievement. Trends over time provide policy-makers with information not only on how the achievement levels of students in their country change in comparison with the achievement levels of students in other countries, but also on how within-country differences, such as gender gaps in achievement, evolve over time. The increasing emphasis on trend indicators has constituted a major change in international surveys of education over the past decade. The names of two current IEA surveys reflect this growing interest: the *Trends* in International Mathematics and Science Study (TIMSS), and the *Progress* in International Reading Literacy Study (PIRLS).

Under IRT assumptions, the same linking function should be obtained regardless of which common items are used because item-specific properties are fully accounted for by the item's IRT parameters. However, model misspecifications always occur, and no model fits real data perfectly. Factors contributing to misfit include small changes in the items, position effects, test design, and curriculum effects. This misfit means other sets of linked items can generate other linking transformations, even with very large examinee samples. According to Michaelides and Haertel (2004), error due to common-item sampling depends not on the size of the examinee sample but on the number of common items used. As such, the error due to the common-item sampling could constitute the dominant source of error for summary scores.

Although IEA reports trends indicators for achievement in its current studies, the association bases the standard error reported for the trends estimates only on the standard errors associated with the two mean achievement estimates used to compute the trends. This trend standard error estimate has two components—the sampling uncertainty and the measurement uncertainty. It therefore consists of (i) sampling variance and (ii) uncertainty about student performance, and it is reflected through the variance of the plausible values. In contrast, the PISA 2003 initial report, which also reports trends indicators in reading, adds another source of variance. As described in the PISA 2003 technical report (Organisation for Economic Co-operation and Development/OECD, 2005), the standard error on the trends estimates contains a third error component, denoted as the linking error. This error reflects model misfit, such as item parameter drift, between the two data collections. However, the linking error, as used in PISA 2003, appears to be unsatisfactory because:

1. It assumes item independency, which is inconsistent with the embedded structure of items into units (passages or blocks of items);

2. It requires that partial credit items be considered dichotomous items; and

3. It takes only the international misspecifications between the two data collections into account.

This situation can lead to researchers underestimating the linking errors and thus increasing the Type I error. This situation, in turn, results in researchers reporting a significant change in achievement when, in fact, the change may not be significant. Furthermore, researchers generally interpret and publish results without regard to the test used. In other words, IEA reports achievement results in terms of reading literacy, mathematics, and science in general and not in terms of, for example, reading literacy on a specific test, such as with the PIRLS test. It also appears to interpret an achievement trend in terms of change in the student performance and not in terms of change in achievement on the anchoring items. In this context, the political importance of trends in achievement should not be underestimated. Also, if scholars suggest educational reforms based on the significant shifts, they may actually end up offering inappropriate policy recommendations.

Throughout the history of international surveys of achievement in education, the IEA Reading Literacy Study has offered a unique opportunity to study the linking error. This is because the achievement test used in 2003 is exactly the same as the achievement test used in the IEA Reading Literacy Study of 1991. In other surveys, instruments differ, changes in the test design occur, and/or (as is the case in PISA) the relative importance of the domains vary from one data collection to another.

METHOD

Nine countries participated in both the IEA Reading Literacy Study 1991 and the Reading Literacy Repeat Study 2001. However, the data from only eight countries were reanalyzed (Greece, Hungary, Iceland, Italy, New Zealand, Slovenia, Sweden, and the United States). It was not possible to include the data from Singapore because these were unavailable at the time of analysis.

The Reading Literacy Study 1991 performance instrument consisted of 106 items administered to all students, without any rotation (Wolf, 1995). The first 40 items, which assessed "*word recognition*," were not included in our study.

> The Word Recognition part was followed by a number of reading passages and documents, for each of which a set of items were asked. Four reading passages with 22 items were selected from the expository domain, five passages with 21 items were selected from the expository domain, and six documents with 23 items were selected from the documents domain. (Elley, 1994, p. 10)

Two of the 66 items were deleted because they had been recoded "*not applicable*" for all students in a country.[1] We therefore had a pool of 64 items from which we could randomly select particular numbers of items.

We decided not to pursue alternatives, such as resampling methods based on the jackknife procedure, because the main focus of our study was (i) to empirically demonstrate the existence of a linking error, (ii) to analyze the significance of reporting

---

[1]   The original test consisted of 68 items but two were deleted at the international level.

a common linking error for all countries, and (iii) to show the effect of anchor-test length on the linking error. However, the method of randomly selecting items from the pool that we adopted in this paper did not take into account the embedded structure of the test, that is, the set of items related to a single reading passage. Further, because we selected items from a finite pool of 64 items, the empirical linking error automatically became 0 when the number of selected concurrently calibrated items was equal to the whole set of items, namely the 64 in the case under consideration.

Let us suppose, then, that 20 items of the 64 were used in the IEA Reading Literacy 2001 study. This would have resulted in about 28 millions of billions of possible different tests from the 20 items out of the pool of 64 items. For this study, we constructed 50 tests of 20 items randomly selected from the item pool. We used the same method to construct 50 tests of 30 items, 50 tests of 40 items, and 50 tests of 50 items. We used ConQuest (Wu, Adams, & Wilson, 1997) to analyze each data set (i.e., eight countries by two data collections by 50 tests by four types of tests, or 3,200 data sets) and thereby draw plausible values.

Note that we did not use conditioning variables. The absence of conditioning enlarges the variance of the *posterior* distributions and therefore slightly increases the imputation error. It also underestimates the relationship between contextual variables and performance. However, because we mainly analyzed the difference in the country mean estimates between two data collections, we determined that any bias introduced through the absence of conditioning was acceptable given the additional computation time that a more sophisticated model would necessitate.

Before generating the plausible values, we drew random samples of 500 students per country and per data collection, and performed a joint calibration of the whole item pool so as to obtain the item parameters according to a one-parameter IRT model. We then transformed the plausible values on the *logit* scale on a new scale with a mean of 500 and a standard deviation of 100 by using *senate* weight per test, whatever the number of items included in the test. Thus, the distribution of the eight countries and the two data collections had a mean of 500 and a standard deviation of 100. We then computed the achievement trend per test by comparing the country mean at Time 1 (1991) and the country mean at Time 2 (2001). Finally, we computed the mean and the standard deviation of the 50 trends estimated for each type of test.

RESULTS

The average trends per type of test all correlated at 0.97 and are reported in the international report (Martin, Mullis, Gonzalez, & Kennedy, 2003). We could not expect a perfect correlation because Singapore was not included in the analyses. Also, the scaling model in this approach (1PL) differed from the model used in the 10-year trend study (3PL).

---

[2] Here, the sum of the student weights per country and per data collection is a constant, which means that each country contributed equally to the linear transformation.

Table 1 and Figure 1 present the linking error, that is, the standard deviation across the 50 trends estimates per type of test. As the table and figure show, the trend estimate for a particular country varies according to the selection of anchor items. For example, with tests of 20 items, the trends estimates for Greece range from 22 to 52. These results clearly demonstrate the impact of the item selection on the trend estimates and advocate the use of a linking error for testing the significance level of a particular trend. Because, in international surveys, the link between two data collections usually is based on fewer than 40 items, the linking error is quite substantial, and it is more or less the same size as the sampling error. For instance, the standard errors on the achievement trend estimates in PIRLS 2001 (Martin et al., 2003) ranged from 3.7 to 7.4. No doubt, the outcomes of the test would differ for countries with low trend estimates.

Table 1: Linking error (i.e., standard deviation of the 50 trend estimates) per country and per type of test

	GRC	HUN	ISL	ITA	NZL	SVN	SWE	USA
Test of 20 items	6.78	4.88	5.16	4.11	4.51	5.52	5.64	4.6
Test of 30 items	5.74	3.57	3.41	3.24	2.79	4.00	3.83	3.54
Test of 40 items	3.15	2.76	2.67	2.21	2.13	2.97	3.07	2.56
Test of 50 items	2.15	1.85	2.05	1.53	2.00	2.00	2.08	1.84

Figure 1: Linking error per country and per type of test

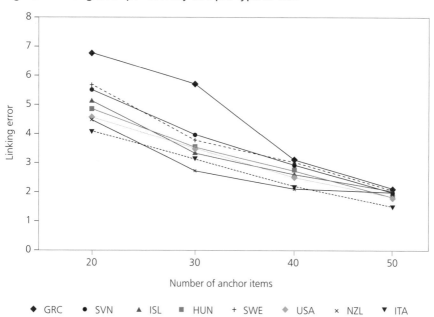

How do these empirical linking errors compare with the analytic solution adopted in the PISA 2000 technical report (Adams & Wu, 2002)? Here, we computed the variability of the shift in item parameters between their 1991 estimates and their 2001 estimates and then transformed them on the IEA Reading Literacy scale. On using Formula 1 (below), we found the linking error was equal to 4.2 for a test with 20 anchor items, to 3.4 for a test with 30 anchor items, to 3.0 for a test with 40 anchor items, and to 2.7 for a test with 50 anchor items.

$$\sigma_{(linking)} = \sqrt{\frac{\sigma^2_{(shift)}}{n_{(anchor)}}}$$

(1)

Because the method we adopted in this paper assumes a finite population of items, and because Formula 1 assumes an infinite population of items, the empirical linking error estimate and the analytical linking error estimate do not converge as the number of anchor items increases. However, the inconsistencies between the two estimates for a small number of items are noticeable. The analytical solution apparently underestimates the linking error. Table 1 and Figure 1 also show the variability of the linking error from one country to another for a particular test type. For example, the linking error is 6.78 for Greece but only 4.11 for Italy. This observation implies that a single linking error for all countries was not as accurate as it should have been.

Why do some countries present a larger linking error? As shown in Table 2, the size of the linking error correlates highly with the importance of the trends estimates. We can expect this observation to some extent because the posterior variance is greatest at the extremes, but this is not the case if the test is targeted to the most proficient or the least proficient populations. Furthermore, if the linking error varies at the country level, we could expect the linking error to also vary across sub-populations within countries. As an illustration, Figure 2 presents the linking error per country and per gender for a test of 20 items.

Table 2: Correlation between the trend estimate (expressed in absolute value) and its linking error

Type of test	Correlation
20	0.91
30	0.88
40	0.82
50	0.66

Figure 2: Overall linking error for 20-item linking and linking error by gender

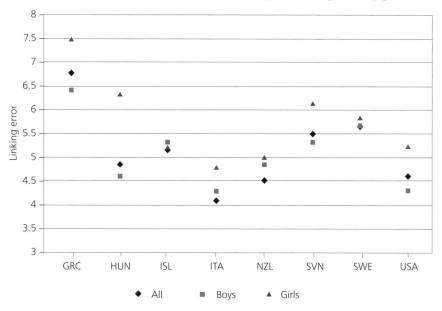

Our analysis thus far has identified two factors influencing the size of the linking error. The first is the number of items and the second is the size of the trends. But we also need to consider two other factors—the embedded structure of the items and the modification in the test design.

Most of the PISA and the IEA Reading Literacy and PIRLS assessment materials present a hierarchical structure: items are clustered in units. A unit consists of a stimulus, that is, a reading passage in the case of the Reading Literacy assessment and a contextualization for the PISA mathematics and science literacy assessment, followed by a set of items all related to that stimulus. By adapting Formula 1 to a cluster sample, we obtain, in the case of a constant number of items per unit, the following:

$$\sigma_{(linking)} = \sqrt{\frac{\sigma^2_{(between\_unit\_shift)}}{n_{(anchor\_unit)}} + \frac{\sigma^2_{(within\_unit\_shift)}}{n_{(anchor\_unit)}}}$$

Monseur and Berezner (2006) reported a substantial increase of the linking error with items organized in units. These authors also have analyzed, through simulations, the accuracy of a jackknifing method and analytical solution for estimating the linking error with hierarchically structured items. The analytical solution and the jackknife methods provide estimates that do not significantly differ from the empirical estimates of the linking error.

A change in the test design constitutes the second additional factor that can affect the size of the linking error. The IEA Reading Literacy study is of particular interest in this regard, as no changes were made in the test instruments. We used a variance decomposition with three factors—country, item, and time—to analyze the national item parameters from a one-parameter IRT model. Because the items are centered for any country at any time, the time variance, the country variance, and the time-by-country interaction variance are equal to 0.

We also conducted this analysis on the PISA anchor reading items between the 2000 and the 2003 data collections. The PISA 2000 test design consisted of nine tests, with four blocks of items for each test. The 28 anchor items appeared only in the first three blocks. In 2003, these 28 items were distributed into two clusters of reading items and appeared once in each of the four positions.

Table 3 presents the estimation of the variance components. Here we can see that in the IEA Reading Literacy study, the time-by-item interaction is about one third of the time-by-item-by-country interaction. However, in PISA, the time-by-item interaction is about twice the value of the time-by-item-by-country interaction. A modification in the test design can therefore have marked consequences for the size of the linking error. This last observation should encourage test developers of international surveys in education to avoid, or at least minimize, changes in the test design between two data collections.

Table 3: Variance decomposition of the national item parameter

Source of variation	IEA Reading Literacy	OECD PISA
Item	1.02590	0.95443
Country by item	0.17701	0.14794
Time by item	0.01083	0.04040
Time by item by country	0.03090	0.02758

CONCLUSION

In 2004, the PISA 2003 initial report published by the Organisation for Economic Co-operation and Development (OECD, 2004) reported trends. As described in the OECD PISA 2003 technical report (OECD, 2005), the standard error of the trend estimate included a linking error. However, as Monseur and Berezner (2006) pointed out, the addition of a linking component in the standard error in the study constituted a methodological improvement but did raise several issues. Essentially, the linking error as used in PISA 2003 seemed unsatisfactory for the same reasons as those outlined in the introduction to this paper.

The results of the simulations presented in this study highlight the relationship between the number of items and the linking error and (more importantly) the variability of the linking error from one country to another. The linking error also correlated highly with the achievement trend estimates. The results additionally highlight the increase in the linking error for within-country analyses as shown by the gender example. Finally, the analyses presented in this paper outline the danger of modifying the test design on the linking error.

Further analyses should now be devoted to computing the linking error on the final set of anchoring items. Replication methods like jackknifing and bootstrapping usually used in the sampling area might be of interest. While an analytical solution might be adopted for simple contexts, jackknifing presents no restriction. It can be used with two- or three-parameter IRT models, with polytomous items, and with hierarchically structured items where units do not necessarily have the same number of items.

If policy-makers and international report readers limited their interpretation of the trend estimates to the anchoring items, it would not be necessary to recommend the addition of a linking error. However, an improvement in student performance based on several dozen anchor-items is currently interpreted by researchers and policy-makers as an improvement in student performance for the whole domain assessed by the study. As such, the inclusion of a linking error in reporting trends would be consistent with how trends are presently interpreted.

According to Michaelides and Haertel (2004), common items should be considered as chosen from a hypothetical infinite pool of potential items. Cronbach, Linn, Brennan, and Haertel (1997) also adhere to this point of view. Remember that a test score is based on an examinee's performance on a particular test form consisting of certain items. What is therefore of most interest is not how well the examinee did on those particular items at that particular occasion. Rather, it is the inference drawn from that example of performance to what the examinee could do across many other tasks requiring the application of the same skills and knowledge.

The interpretations of the trends indicators by policy-makers and the arguments presented by scholars like Michaelides and Haertel and Cronbach and colleagues advocate hypothetical infinite populations. In other words, even if a new international test did include all items from a previous survey, a linking error would still need to be reported. This linking error would reflect the model misspecifications.

Limitations of the current research are that we used only two cycles of a reading assessment, and that we could compute only linking errors for true subsets of the anchor test. However, the research presented here demonstrates that linking error is a potential source of variation that can be quantified through computational procedures involving resampling methods, such as the bootstrap and the jackknife (Efron, 1982). Future research could focus on methods that take linking error as well as sampling error into account simultaneously. One way of doing this is outlined in Cohen, Johnson, and Angeles (2001). However, their approach to jackknifing in two dimensions needs careful examination in terms of whether it is executed correctly and yields appropriate variance estimates. But whether executed as identifying separable sources, or whether carried out simultaneously, research that incorporates additional tractable sources of variation promises to improve comparisons both across and within countries for subgroups of interest to policy-makers and educators.

References

Adams, R. J., & Wu, M. (Eds.). (2002). *PISA 2000 technical report*. Paris: Organisation for Economic Co-operation and Development.

Cohen, J., Johnson, E., & Angeles, J. (2001). *Estimates of the precision of estimates from NAEP using a two-dimensional jackknife procedure*. Paper presented at the annual meeting of the National Council of Measurement in Education, Seattle, WA.

Cronbach, L. J., Linn, R. L., Brennan, R. L., & Haertel, E. H. (1997). Generalizability analysis for performance assessments of student achievement or school effectiveness. *Educational and Psychological Measurement, 57*, 373–399.

Efron, B. (1982). The jackknife, the bootstrap and other resampling plans. *Society of Industrial and Applied Mathematics CBMS-NSF Monographs*, No. 38.

Elley, W. B. (1994). *The IEA study of reading literacy: Achievement and instruction in thirty-two school systems*. London: Pergamon.

Martin, M. O., Mullis, I. V. S., Gonzalez, E. J., & Kennedy, A. M. (2003). *PIRLS trends in children's reading literacy achievement 1991–2001*. Chestnut Hill, MA: Boston College.

Michaelides, M. P., & Haertel, E. H. (2004). *Sampling of common items: An unrecognized source of error in test linking*. Los Angeles: Center for the Study of Evaluation (CSE), University of California.

Monseur, C., & Berezner, A. (2006). *The computation of linking error*. Paper presented at the AERA annual convention's symposium on measuring trends in international comparative research: Results from the first two cycles of the OECD/PISA study, San Francisco.

Organisation for Economic Co-operation and Development (OECD). (2004). *Learning for tomorrow's world: First results from PISA 2003*. Paris: Author.

Organisation for Economic Co-operation and Development (OECD). (2005). *PISA 2003 technical report*. Paris: Author.

Wolf, R. M. (1995). *The IEA Reading Literacy study: Technical report*. The Hague: International Association for the Evaluation of Educational Achievement.

Wu, M. L., Adams, R. J., & Wilson, M. R. (1997). *ConQuest: Multi-aspect test software* (computer program). Camberwell, VIC: Australian Council for Educational Research.

INFORMATION FOR CONTRIBUTORS

Content

IERI Monograph Series: Issues and Methodologies in Large-Scale Assessments is a joint publication between the International Association for the Evaluation of Educational Achievement (IEA) and Educational Testing Service (ETS). The goal of the publication is to contribute to the science of large-scale assessments so that the best available information is provided to policy-makers and researchers from around the world. Papers accepted for this publication are those that focus on improving the science of large-scale assessments and that make use of data collected by programs such as IEA-TIMSS, IEA-PIRLS, IEA-Civics, IEA-SITES, US-NAEP, OECD-PISA, OECD-PIAAC, IALS, ALL, etc.

If you have questions or concerns about whether your paper adheres to the purpose of the series, please contact us at IERInstitute@iea-dpc.de.

Style

The style guide for all IERI publications is the *Publication Manual of the American Psychological Association* (5th ed., 2001). Manuscripts should be typed on letter or A4 format, upper and lower case, double spaced in its entirety, with one-inch margins on all sides. The type size should be 12 point. Subheads should be at reasonable intervals to break the monotony of lengthy text. Pages should be numbered consecutively at the bottom of the page, beginning with the page after the title page. Mathematical symbols and Greek letters should be clearly marked to indicate italics, boldface, superscript, and subscript.

Please submit all manuscripts electronically, preferably in MS-Word format and with figures and tables in editable form (e.g., Word, Excel) to the editorial team at IERInstitute@iea-dpc.de and attach the Manuscript Submission Form, which can be obtained from the IERI website: www.ierinstitute.org. For specific questions or inquiries, send emails to editors at the same address. Only electronic submissions are accepted.

Author Identification

The complete title of the article and the name of the author(s) should be typed only on the submission form to ensure anonymity in the review process. The pages of the paper should have no author names, but may carry a short title at the top. Information in the text or references that would identify the author should be deleted from the manuscript (e.g., text citations of "my previous work," especially when accompanied by a self-citation; a preponderance of the author's own work in the reference list). These may be reinserted in the final draft. The author (whether first-named or co-author) who will be handling the correspondence with the editor and working with the publications people should submit complete contact information, including a full mailing address, telephone number, and email addresses.

Review Process

Papers will be acknowledged by the managing editor upon receipt. After a preliminary internal editorial review by IERI staff, articles will be sent to two external reviewers who have expertise in the subject of the manuscript. The review process takes anywhere from three to six months. You should expect to hear from the editor within that time regarding the status of your manuscript. IERI uses a blind review system, which means the identity of the authors is not revealed to the reviewers. In order to be published as part of the monograph series, the work will undergo and receive favorable technical, substantive, and editorial review.

Originality of Manuscript and Copyright

Manuscripts are accepted for consideration with the understanding that they are original material and are not under consideration for publication elsewhere.

To protect the works of authors and the institute, we copyright all of our publications. Rights and permissions regarding the uses of IERI-copyrighted materials are handled by the IERI executive board. Authors who wish to use material, such as figures or tables, for which they do not own the copyright must obtain written permission from IERI and submit it to IERI with their manuscripts.

Comments and Grievances

The Publications Committee welcomes comments and suggestions from authors. Please send these to the committee at IERInstitute@iea-dpc.de.

The right-of-reply policy encourages comments on articles recently published in an IERI publication. Such comments are subject to editorial review and decision. If the comment is accepted for publication, the editor will inform the author of the original article. If the author submits a reply to the comment, the reply is also subject to editorial review and decision.

If you think that your manuscript is not reviewed in a careful or timely manner and in accordance with standard practices, please call the matter to the attention of the institute's executive board.

Publication Schedule

There will be one publication per year. This publication will consist of five to seven research papers. Manuscripts will be reviewed and processed as soon as they are received and will be published in the next available monograph series. In the event that, in a single year, there are more than seven accepted manuscripts, the editorial committee will determine whether the manuscript(s) will be published the next year or in an additional monograph in the same year. Manuscripts are accepted any time of the year.